Introduction to the 2nd Edition

This second edition is the "fault" of the thousands of the Bible teachers who have corresponded with me since the first edition was published in 2004. Their questions, suggestions, and insights have confirmed that the basic principles are timeless, and the opportunities remain open worldwide!

It's clear to me now that I've learned more about teaching after I published a book than before. We are ever in the foothills of learning.

You might wonder what's changed in the 2nd edition. In addition to tightening up the editing, I reference online materials that I've created since the original edition. The general structure of a lesson plan is now "hook, key points, application, launch" reflecting what God has been teaching me. I've also expanded the prayer support team section and updated the suggest resources.

May the Lord continue to bless His teachers of His Word!

Glenn Brooke
November 2011

Table of Contents

Why This Book Is For You

Teach the Bible to Change Lives is for those in God's Church that are called to teach others and facilitate small group discussions of Scripture. This book is focused on the specific needs and challenges of teachers. If you have a Bible, this book, and a willing heart to serve the Lord through teaching, you have everything you need to become a great Bible teacher. **My approach develops YOU as the teaching tool God will use**.

You are about to get a jump-start on your teaching – and your personal walk with the Lord – like nothing you've ever encountered before. I'll be your coach and encourager. This book presents a complete package of information for you. My recommended approaches are not the easiest or fastest – but they will put you on a strong course to teach the Bible to change lives. Changing lives is what counts. (See 1 Corinthians 3:5-9).

There are four key elements necessary to change lives through your Bible teaching. Great Bible teachers work at all four. Ordinary teachers only work at one or two of these four elements, and then they're often disappointed with the results.

4

If you look at how Moses, Jesus, and Paul taught people, you'll see all four elements at work. I'm confident that you are going to get great ideas for teaching even before you finish this book.

For the purpose of this book, I am assuming that you are teaching an adult Sunday School class. The information in this book is valuable for teaching young people, singles, married couples, and seniors. Nearly all of these ideas apply to teaching in any setting – large groups, small group settings, and within your home! (Appendix 2 describes how to adapt this material for different kinds of teaching situations.)

My prayer is that our Lord will use the information in this e-book to develop and encourage a new and much larger group of great – not merely adequate, not just competent, but **GREAT** -- Bible teachers.

Teaching is an important responsibility (see James 3:1). Therefore, do not listen to counsel about teaching unless it is godly and consistent with the Bible. It's vitally important that this book be true to Scripture. I believe it is. Paul admonishes us to "test everything" (1 Thessalonians 5:21) – you should be like the Bereans (Acts 17:11) and check what I say against the Word of God.

It's important that you understand my statement of faith and have confidence that my counsel is sound. I am an evangelical Christian. I have been teaching adult Sunday School classes for over 25 years. I subscribe to the 10 points of doctrine of the Evangelical Free Church. See "About the Author" near the end of this book for additional details.

Are you ready? Let's get on with the material. The next section describes what distinguishes Great Bible teachers and gives an overview of the key elements that change lives through Bible teaching.

Great Bible Teachers Use Four Key Elements to Change Lives

What Distinguishes a Great Bible Teacher?

The Church today is crying out for Bible teaching. We desperately need men and women who can help people hear God's voice and obey it. I believe God is already working to raise up a whole new generation of teachers to prepare His people for works of service and increase the praise to His glorious Name. There are great revivals coming, friends, and more and more teachers will be needed to help these new believers.

First, there is the quantity concern. There are many teachers, but few teach the Truth. I believe that the days Paul describes in 2 Timothy 4:3-4 are here. "For the time will come when men will not put up with sound doctrine. Instead, to suit their own desires, they will gather around them a great number of teachers to say what their itching ears want to hear. They will

7

turn their ears away from the truth and turn aside to myths."
And Hosea 4:6 also rings with truth for our time: "my people
are destroyed from lack of knowledge."

A simple scan of television stations and bookstores will
confirm that there are many teachers available who will tell
you the "secrets" of whatever you're interested in. We're
lacking enough teachers who competently use the Scriptures
as their source matter.

Then there is the quality concern. The Church (particularly in
the United States) is trending towards shallow faith and
biblical illiteracy. We are turning out more and more poorly-
equipped "greenhouse" Christians who only know how to
honor and serve the Lord under controlled conditions and no
stress. We do not want to produce "biblical cripples" who are
dependent on someone else to listen to God through His Word
and tell them what to do. These are wonderful days for
service for the Glory of Jesus Christ, and so we need many
strong Christians.

Bible teaching is critical to reversing this decline. I am
confident that a key element to strengthening God's people is
the diligent service of men and women who know the Word of
God, know how to teach it, and love people.

What makes for a Great Bible teacher? How are Great Bible teachers different than other teachers? **Great Bible teachers are conduits of the love of God for people!** Great Bible Teachers:

- Have energy and passion for the Word of God and for prayer
- Always purpose to grow in knowledge of the Word, both breadth and depth
- Focus on the needs of their students, love them and desire to see them becoming spiritually mature
- See students as disciples, learners, future missionaries and Kingdom workers, each one a worshipper of the Almighty God of the Bible
- Are skilled at getting a class engaged in discussion – small or large -- and excited enough to continue to think about a lesson for days and weeks later
- Teach boldly, knowing that God desires to transform both hearts and minds
- Can either create new teaching content, breaking new ground, or adapt existing content to the needs of a specific group

- Do not merely echo what others have taught – they teach powerfully from the authentic character of Christ that is formed in them
- Never stop learning

Some of you may be reading that phrase "Great Bible teacher" and think I'm recommending that teachers puff themselves up and draw attention to their "super ministry." Absolutely not! Great Bible teachers are humble and recognize that they serve only one Master, and using the gifts and provision that He has provided for this very purpose.

I'm going to use the acronym GBT for <u>G</u>reat <u>B</u>ible <u>T</u>eacher in the rest of this book.

I have a passionate, prayerful dream of a Church with an increasing number of GBTs building up the body and training the next generation of GTBs. These GBTs will have minimal dependence on anything except the Word of God and the Holy Spirit, seeking to wrestle with the Word to bring precisely what God's people need. These GBTs bathe their teaching in prayer – before, during, and after class. This is a generation of GBTs that sees their teaching as a primary ministry to the people within the sphere the Lord has established for them to influence.

We need tens of thousands of GBTs to "make disciples of all nations…and teaching them to obey everything I have commanded you." (Matthew 28:20)

You can be a GBT. You can learn to teach like Jesus (see Mark 12:14). I believe that God is sovereign and this book has not come into your hands by accident or fate. There is a strong message here for you. "The fields are white for harvest; pray, therefore that the Lord of the harvest will send workers." (Matt 9:37-38) That's you. Our Lord has a place for you, and is going to give you an enormous spiritual legacy.

A friend gave me this suggested acronym after reading an early draft of this book:

G   God-responsive

R   Recognizes class needs

E   Excellent preparation

A   Application-oriented

T   Theologically sound/teachable

Amen! I'd use this, but another author has already written extensively using a slightly different acronym for GREAT.

Apollos was a GBT

24Meanwhile a Jew named Apollos, a native of Alexandria, came to Ephesus. He was a learned man, with a thorough knowledge of the Scriptures. 25He had been instructed in the way of the Lord, and he spoke with great fervor and taught about Jesus accurately, though he knew only the baptism of John. 26He began to speak boldly in the synagogue. When Priscilla and Aquila heard him, they invited him to their home and explained to him the way of God more adequately.

27When Apollos wanted to go to Achaia, the brothers encouraged him and wrote to the disciples there to welcome him. On arriving, he was a great help to those who by grace had believed. 28For he vigorously refuted the Jews in public debate, proving from the Scriptures that Jesus was the Christ. -- Acts 18:24-28, NIV

Apollos is one of my heroes. Apollos is a great model teacher for us to imitate – one of the earliest GBTs! He was a learned man, with a thorough knowledge of the Scriptures (v. 24).

Other translations say he was "mighty" in the Scriptures – there's a great picture of an effective teacher! We should devote ourselves to learning, absorbing, and understanding the Bible.

He spoke with great fervor (v. 25) and boldness (v. 26). That's another key for great Bible teaching – heart-inflamed passion and bold speaking.

But note that Apollos has a teachable spirit, too. (v. 26) He receives instruction from Priscilla and Aquila. And consider how blessed Apollos was that they took this opportunity to help him – we need to look for opportunities to help other teachers.

Apollos' teaching changes lives – he was "a great help to those who by grace had believed" (v.27) – and yet it is God who gets the credit. Apollos had the right perspective that he was only a tool being used by God.

The focus of Apollos' teaching was Jesus, and the basis for his teaching was the Bible. (v. 28) And so it must be with us today if we are to honor the Lord. May our gracious God and

King raise up thousands of GBTs like Apollos to build up His Church today.

The Four Key Elements

Here is a diagram illustrating the four key elements that God works together to change lives:

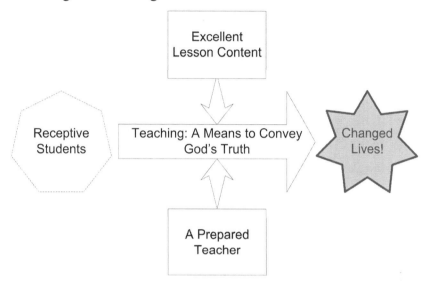

Our goal as Bible teachers is <u>Changed Lives</u>, and we should aim for nothing less. We cooperate with God to achieve this through powerful, God-saturated teaching! We work to become GBTs to meet the needs before us. The days are short, and there is much work to be done.

Great teaching depends upon four critical elements:

1. **Excellent Lesson Content.** There is nothing superior to the Bible, the God-breathed truth (2 Timothy 3:16-17). Week in, week out, your students need to receive instruction, correction, and training that comes directly from the Bible. Nothing else can consistently meet their deepest needs. Nothing else has God-given authority for teaching men and women how to live. (See Matthew 7:29 about the crowd's amazement at Jesus' teaching.)

2. **A Prepared Teacher**. God uses men and women to teach the truth. He has given us everything we need in the Church to help us to grow. Preparation includes prayer, Bible study and meditation, and an effective presentation.

3. **Receptive Students.** The lesson needs a place to land and take root if there are going to be changed lives. Only God can prepare a heart to receive His teaching. We cannot do this on our own – we must prayerfully invite the Lord of the universe to prepare the hearts of those who will hear a lesson. (Consider Mark 4:1-20)

4. **Teaching is a means to convey God's truth.**
   Teaching is a process. Teaching is a kind of
   leadership. Teaching is really about loving people and
   wanting to see them grow and mature.

What Do Changed Lives Look Like?

The old saying is true: "If you don't know where you're
going, any road will take you there." We have to understand
what kind of changed life we're talking about! **Your students
are not only looking for information, but for
transformation.** They need to taste and see that the Lord is
good (Psalm 34:8)

I use 2 Peter 3:18 as the benchmark. "But grow in the grace
and knowledge of our Lord and Savior Jesus Christ." **A
changed life means that there is growth in grace and in
knowledge of Jesus.** For not-yet believers, that means
salvation. For everyone, it means changes in thinking and
behavior. The fact that it is both growth in grace and
knowledge distinguishes Christians from everyone else on
Earth. (C.S. Lewis pointed out that no other religion has
anything that corresponds to the Christian concept of Grace.)

There is no age or gender specified – growth is open to all. Note also the strong community of faith element here: Peter says "*our* Lord and Savior," not "my" or "your" Lord and Savior. Genuine Christian growth takes place in fellowship, in community. Your teaching ministry is key.

Jesus said, "It is enough for the student to be like his teacher, and the servant like his master." (Matthew 10:25) We should expect that disciples, growing in grace and knowledge of Jesus, look more and more like Him.

Growing in grace and knowledge of Jesus affects both heart and head.

Growth in grace of Jesus means that our character is more Christ-like. We are more patient, kind, joyful, and gentle with one another. We exhibit self-control and all the fruits of the Spirit (Galatians 5:22). Our trust in God and obedience to His commands deepens. Other people cannot mistake that there is something different about us!

Growth in knowledge of Jesus means our minds are more fitted to accurately understand ourselves, our culture, and our Lord. We have information plus the ability to use it for service for our Master. We know how to apply the truths and

18

principles of Scripture to everyday life. We are equipped to use the Word of God in ministry.

The end result is that people are changed. They

- Know how to listen to God's voice and obey it
- Offer their lives in worship (Romans 12:1)
- Have renewed minds, able to test and approve God's will (Romans 12:2)
- Are competent to pass on what they know, to this generation and the next

Bible-based teaching plays a critical role in growth for both grace and knowledge. As we invest time in God's Word our characters and minds are transformed. GBTs are humble, remembering that God uses us, but it is up to Him to provide the growth. (1 Corinthians 3:6-7) We pray that we help rather than hinder the work of God, confident that our Lord can – and sometimes does – work in spite of us. Teaching is a high calling of cooperating with God's fellow servants to facilitate change in others.

Not all students are at the same place now, nor will all have the same growth rate. This reality shapes how we approach a class, and helps us remain patient as God works His change in people's hearts and minds.

All this requires absolute dependence upon God! GBTs are called to faithfully present information, and call upon God to see the growth in grace and knowledge of Jesus. Changed lives are the fruit from our cooperation with God in teaching ministry. GBTs are leaders and encouragers, not standing in judgment over students. Our Lord is caring for His sheep.

How This Book Is Organized

Teach The Bible To Change Lives is designed to help those whom God calls to teach to prepare lessons and teach the Bible in a way that changes lives. This is serious work, but a blessed calling! May God raise up strong teachers to match the great need in His Church today, so that the next generations may also give praise and honor to the Lord. Amen!

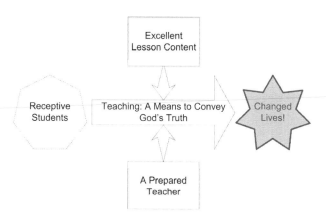

This book is laid out in six main parts. Parts I through IV correspond to the four elements in the diagram above. The reality is that that GBTs will work in several of these areas at the same time. Part V walks you through a practical example of putting all these elements together. Part VI is about follow-up work that is essential for teachers.

I suspect you're eager to skip ahead to Part IV (Teaching) and Part V (Putting It All Together), but I encourage you to walk through this book in sequence. Let's begin with excellent lesson content.

Part I: Excellent Lesson Content

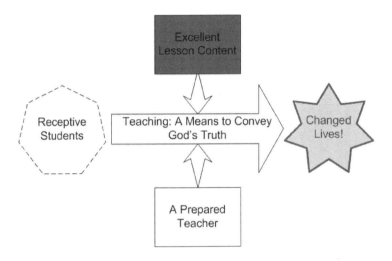

We begin by answering the question "What are you going to teach?"

A GBT will respond this way: **"I will teach what the Lord desires these people to learn about at this time."** That's the only way to approach this question if we're going to be part of God's plan to change lives.

We must understand the needs of the people – at both a heart and head level. It means seeking the Lord's guidance. (He teaches us before we can teach others!) It means being able to handle the Word of God in a trustworthy manner (2 Timothy 2:11), so we can create lessons from the Bible itself, with the help of the Holy Spirit. It means being able to recognize when prepared lessons from other sources are a good fit for our students' needs. It means bathing lesson preparation in prayer.

Teaching to change lives is not always easy or comfortable. You may be able to recycle a lesson you've successfully taught before or picked up somewhere, but often not. You can't always stay with familiar Bible texts. You will probably step on a few "toes," just as Jesus did. You must be willing to tackle topics that challenge or stretch you, as well as your students.

It cannot be overemphasized that **the best lesson content always comes from the Bible**. Nothing less than the Word of God can meet every need and satisfy every heart, week after week. Your teaching ministry will have life-changing impact on student when it is based on the Word of God and Prayer – it will not be possible to explain the impact in human terms.

23

Real-World Bible Lessons Don't Begin Fully-Formed

Spiral of Archimedes

Real-world Bible lessons are constructed over time. This is a critical point for GBTs to understand, and is often misunderstood by young teachers. You build up and refine lessons in an iterative fashion. You select the general material, but you may not have the key points identified yet. You get some sense of alignment of this lesson against the needs of your students (much more about this below!), but aren't sure exactly what to emphasize or in what order to present it. It's as if you "spiral in" on the final product. You certainly won't get the information for your lesson ironed out in sequence. So this section is about the early stages of lesson material selection and refinement, not the polishing stages.

Be content with an iterative approach. Be patient. You can't finalize your lesson material until you've spent time studying it and praying through it. God is going to give you life lessons, too, which may not come until late in your lesson preparation. That's ok, because that's how the Lord keeps us in dependence upon Him (see John 15:5).

Three Sources of Lesson Material

There are three basic ways to create a lesson:

1. Create your own lesson from Bible study that you have done.

2. Use or adapt a pre-made lesson someone else has created.

3. Synthesize your own lesson components with a lesson or illustration that someone else has created.

The objective of every GBT is to identify and use material that is best suited to meet the needs of students at this time.

I will begin with discussion about pre-made lessons, and then come back to creating your own lesson.

Let us praise God that there are hundreds or thousands of Bible lessons already in existence! This is a wonderful legacy of a generous Body of Christ through many generations. This is enabling many busy pastors and teachers to bring high-quality information to their students without having to do a lot of original work. My research indicates that about 85% of adult Sunday School classes in the United States are using pre-packaged lesson material. Pre-packaged lessons play an important role in the equipping ministry of our churches.

There's a simple reason that the American church today has only a small fraction of spiritually mature believers even though we're awash in Bible studies: **Lesson content by itself does not result in changed lives!** All the other elements of the GBT teaching model (prepared teacher, receptive students, and quality teaching) are still needed. Frankly, we don't need more Bible study guides (the booklet kind), but we do need many more Bible study guides (the teacher kind).

If you are going to use lesson materials that someone else has developed, then invest your time in prayer, Bible study that corresponds to the lesson, and efforts to prepare your students. We'll be talking about all these things in the sections below. You will have opportunities to surface the needs of these students as you teach and interact with them – that will be important information for future classes. You're still responsible to teach well, so that the truth of God is conveyed.

As you select material that might be appropriate for your students, make sure the lesson content:

1. Demands that students think for themselves and evaluate Scripture for themselves. Sometimes lessons (unintentionally) train people to depend on someone

"really smart and experienced" to understand the Bible and point out what a person should believe. We want to foster the Berean approach of checking the teaching against the Word of God, to see if what the teacher said was true (Acts 17:11).

2. <u>Helps equip the saints for service for the Kingdom (Ephesians 4:12).</u> We are servants of the Lord, and our growth in grace and knowledge of Jesus is to become a better servant and worshiper. We are building up the Body of Christ for ministry work.

3. <u>Is tailored to meet the current needs (not solely the wants) of the students.</u> You want to be able to adjust the emphasis or presentation order or depth to match your local assembly.

Reject lesson material that does not meet these criteria. The Church today is crying out for "men of Issachar, who understood the times and knew what to do." (1 Chronicles 12:32)

I'm very concerned that we develop Christians who are able to create Bible lessons using nothing but the Word of God and the help of the Holy Spirit. Without demeaning the many curricula that are available, I say to you that you can and must do better than a state of dependency on someone else. They don't know your students. God will raise up qualified Bible teachers in local assemblies to equip His people for worship and service. This is absolutely necessary to the generational need in the Church today (see Psalm 78:1-8). If you're reading this book, then it's likely that God is calling you to be a GBT like this.

I do not apologize for my bias in this book towards creating lessons yourself. This is the skill that we need to develop, and that only comes through exercising the gifts the Lord has provided us. At a minimum a GBT must be prepared to enhance or tailor a lesson based on their students' needs by adding from personal Bible study, and effective teaching presentation.

How to Decide What to Teach

Begin with Prayer!

Nothing of eternal value can happen without prayer. Ask the Lord to give you insights into what your hearers need to learn. He knows them and cares for them! As you pray, see yourself as a facilitator so these people can experience more of God. This is not about your agenda, or your ideas, but rather being a faithful servant to the Lord. I like to pray, "Lord, what does this class need to know from this passage at this time? Glorify your name through my teaching." These teaching opportunities are divine appointments. The Lord will bring exactly the right people to each class or study you lead, no one will be there by accident.

Consider Multiple Sources of Input

How are you going to know what to teach a class? That can be a scary question! There are multiple sources of input to consider. Let's explore a few of them, and then I'll give you my recommended strategy.

1. **Explicit guidance from others.**

>Your pastor or church leadership might have a specific topic or book of the Bible they want you to cover. This is often part of a larger curriculum effort. There may not be much more to your decision process, then, about *what* to teach.

2. You might be asked if you have anything ready that you could teach "without a lot of prep time."

>You still have some notes from those other classes you taught, right? ☺. This kind of input becomes common when you're in a church or small group environment where there isn't central planning or a standard curriculum identified.

>But keep in mind what I said earlier about the importance of knowing what the class needs! Don't go with what is easiest for you unless you have other confirmation that this is the BEST for this class at this time.

3. **An idea based on something you've read recently, or heard in a sermon or radio broadcast.**

> GBTs hear or read something and immediately start thinking of how to teach that to their classes. Or how to incorporate an insight, metaphor, or background fact into something they're already working on. This is because GBTs love to teach, and enthused about getting good ideas to their students.

> (By the way, this is one of the reasons you need to take notes in your Bible or journal. You're likely to forget something valuable to share if you don't make a note of it. When driving, I will sometimes pull off the road to make a note.)

4. **A book or topic that God is leading you personally to learn more deeply about.**

> A strong element with this input is that you will have a personal stake in it. There will be stories you can share. Your transparency can

be high – "Hey, this is what God is teaching me about X, and I haven't got all this figured out yet."

Be sure you are ready to teach this topic or book, however. It may well be that God has some more "seasoning" He wants to do in your life before you can teach this one.

5. A need you know about for this specific class.
Is the class all singles? Are there young parents, or parents of teenagers? Perhaps there have been a lot of job or health struggles? Are they 'primed' with interest about a particular spiritual discipline, or eager to tackle an OT book because they've spent most of their time in the NT for two years? What is their heart need? What will help them take greater steps of faith and obedience, for the glory of Jesus Christ? What will enlarge their view of the Lord?

My recommended strategy is simple: look for more than one of these sources of input to line up on a specific book or topic.

My experience has shown me that I need to see God confirming the topic for a class through multiple avenues, or else I risk getting into a situation where I can do no more than increase my pride or tickle someone's ears – lives aren't going to be changed for the better either way. If only one of these inputs is clear, be cautious.

If you ask me to pick one source of input, I'd go with what the class needs. If you are teaching in an area where there is a genuine need, the Lord can work out all kinds of other difficulties so that you can teach to change lives.

In most cases, several of these things will come together and you will be convinced this is God's will for you to proceed. Make sure that you take your idea to the Lord over a several day or week period. I believe that God always speaks clearly and plainly – our problem is faulty hearing and cloudy judgment. Prayerfully considering your planned teaching topic over several days gives you the best confidence that you have heard God's direction correctly. Our loving Father will patiently work with you to ensure His ways are clear.

But what if I'm stumped and don't have any ideas at all?

This can and does happen. The first thing to do is prayerfully give thanks to God for surfacing this and ask Him for guidance. By giving thanks, you immediately work to frustrate prideful or demonic suggestions about what you "should" teach. (I wish I had learned this much earlier in my teaching ministry – and now I've given you a huge jump start!)

The next thing to do is to start asking questions.

Ask the pastor, class leader, and/or some people in the class what kinds of things they think would be valuable to learn about. What have they covered recently?

Talk with the person who was teaching this class previously. What kinds of questions were raised? Was there anything that seemed to need more attention? What excited people? What is the biblical literacy of this class? Did he/she sense there were areas where people needed to grow more?

Here's a list of prompters for questions about your students:

- Relationships (marriage, children, parents, siblings)
- Current local events (political, economic, school system, crimes)
- Deaths or serious illnesses
- Changes in family (new children, aging parents, divorce, adultery)
- New believers
- Faith-testing events (e.g., unemployment)
- Lack of unity in small groups or church
- Concerns for neighbors and coworkers
- Interest in spiritual disciplines
- Outreach possibilities
- Refreshed believers (seeing new growth in old members)

Continue to pray as you consider the answers to these questions. Panic and hurry are neither necessary nor helpful.

Sometimes I sit down in a quiet place and slowly page through my Bible book by book, patiently looking and listening for anything that "jumps out."

Remember that this is God's work, so He is going to lead you to just the right lesson material for this class at this time. Trust in Him, not in any mechanical way to determine "the answer."

Organizing the Lesson

Sturdy, useful buildings need a good foundation. Sturdy, useful Bible study lessons are built on the foundation of the Word and prayer. But what do you build on this foundation? What fundamental elements go into a great lesson?

I'm going to lay out a completely non-secret plan which I use by default; nearly every lesson I've given in over twenty five years of teaching is crafted on this plan. It's repeatable. It's durable. It works. There are only four elements: Hook, Small Number of Focus Points, Life Application, and Launch.

Hook
Begin with a good "hook" to bring people into the lesson, get them hungry for the big meal ahead, and ready for some life-change application to come. Make this as personal as possible for your students. See my free report on creating a powerful hook at http://www.teachtochangelives.com/hooks.pdf

A small number of focus points
My grandfather used to say, "If you don't want people to learn anything, try to teach them everything." (I

doubt he originated this idea.) I'm sure you've been in a situation, maybe a high school or college class, where the teacher just piled on the content and you came away with…nothing. Your brain just shut down when it was overwhelmed. Good teachers work with human psychological realities, not against them -- pick fewer focus points and drill them home.

How many is the right number? That depends on your class. Limit yourself with one to three, my dear GBT, hold yourself in! If there are more items, then pick three for emphasis and only highlight the others. You aren't going to exhaust the depth of Scripture in any lesson, so there's no cause to feel badly about not covering it all.

You want to engage the class to discover these focus points by asking good questions. Where possible, illustrate these focus points by stories, props, and metaphors.

Life Application
"All Scripture is God-breathed and is useful for teaching, rebuking, correcting and training in

righteousness, so that the man of God may be thoroughly equipped for every good work." (2 Timothy 3:16-17) The revealed Word of God will have an impact on us, and not return empty to the Speaker. (Isaiah 55:11) GBTs teach for changed lives, not just piling on head knowledge that does not also affect our hearts and actions.

Identify at least one life application messages for your students. Usually the best way to communicate the life application is in the context of a focus area, rather than a separate point in time. I break it out because I want to think carefully about life application and not overlook its importance. (There will be more about life application in a later section.)

Launch

Wrap up the package and make it easy to take home – or take to heart. This is often a quick summary with a final challenge to further growth in Christ. Sometimes an open-ended question or thought for reflection through the week.

I used to call this the "closer," but switched to the mindset of "launching" my students into ministry. I often say as I invite them to join me in a "closing" prayer, "Let me launch you out of here." The launch mindset really, really helps drive the application home!

That's it. Hook, small number of focus points, life application, and launch.

When it's done right, my students didn't identify the different building blocks – they just flowed and worked together. But every student should have one or two take-aways that Christ can use to change their life. They don't leave saying, "Wow, wasn't Glenn's opener great today? Best hook he's had for months." They leave thinking about the application, or at least some new understanding of biblical truth.

* * * * *

You have a preliminary idea of what God desires you to teach this class at this time. And you have some early ideas about key focus areas, life application, and perhaps an opener and closer. You're moving forward. Now we kick in serious study and preparation.

Part II: A Prepared Teacher

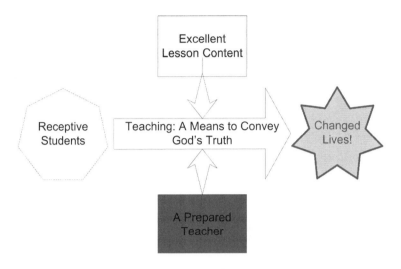

In this section we'll focus on **your preparation for teaching**. Having decided on lesson content, you need to study and prepare yourself to convey God's truth for this class at this time. There are tools and methods that can help you do this.

Studying the Bible in order to teach it to others is very rewarding – you'll learn more than your students! Once you know that you'll be teaching something, your attention will be ten-fold more focused and persistent – that's simply human nature. Studying the Bible for teaching is also different than personal Bible study. The responsibilities and expectations are high. God will not leave you or forsake you, friend. He will be your blessed Guide. Our Lord is our Master, Savior, Teacher, and Friend. You can trust him. The Holy Spirit is our enabler (1 Corinthians 2).

By the time you finish this section, you should have a whole new set of ideas to help you become a GBT. Everything I describe in this section is designed to put you into a place where you will be cooperating with God to be prepared to teach. That's the key.

Tools

The reality is that **YOU are the 'tool' that God will use**. So this section is really about tools or resources you can use to be more effective.

Your one essential tool is a Bible

A simple Bible with a small concordance and cross-references is adequate for 90% of your needs as a teacher. Let me say that again, because it's your most important take-away from this section of the book: A simple Bible with a small concordance and cross-references is adequate for 90% of your needs as a teacher.

The Bible I use every day is a wide-margin NIV Bible from Zondervan. It has plenty of margin space for notes, single column format, a large enough font that I can easily read it in public and keep my place. It includes a decent sized concordance, and a basic set of maps. (I do wish it had is more cross-references.) After wearing out the bindings of several hardbound Bibles I invested in a leather-bound version – it's softening up nicely with regular use.

The wide margins make it easy to take notes directly in the Bible and I use it as my primary tool when teaching. I have plenty of writing space in the back notes pages to include

- sermon notes
- summaries from studies I've done
- a photocopy of my Bible reading plan
- prayer requests for people close to me and for whom I have a special prayer burden
- great quotes that I can use sometime in the future
- outlines of short devotionals I can use in many situations (I'll describe more about this in a later section titled, "Short Lessons on Short Notice")

The habit of capturing notes and materials directly into my Bible creates an increasingly valuable resource to use when teaching or leading groups. So mark up your Bible with pen and pencil. Put dates next to verses and passages that are strongly speaking to you. Underline key passages. Circle words and phrases. Here's a scan of Galatians 6 from my Bible:

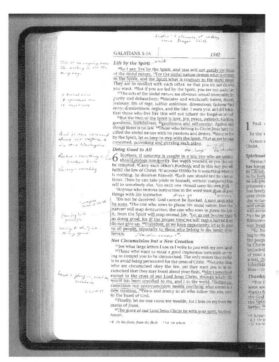

Make it your ambition to wear out Bibles from use! Leave them as a legacy to give to your children. They will treasure your worn, note-studded Bible as a great reminder of your faithfulness that lights their way. If there were a fire in my home and I could grab just one material thing, it would probably be my Bible.

I'm frequently asked " hat about using a Study Bible?" There are plenty to choose from – it seems every possible market for children, youth, men, women, different theological backgrounds, and recovering addicts, to name a few, has a study Bible available. And when my prayers are answered and God raises up a mighty generation of GBTs, will I recommend Bible publishers create a new study Bible just for teachers? No. Let me explain why.

Study Bibles, in my opinion, can get in the way of thoughtful reading and reflection. I've observed that people spend as much time looking at footnotes as the actual text of God's word! Therefore I recommend that people *not* use a study Bible with all the footnotes and helps as their regular reading Bible when preparing to teach. Instead, **use study Bibles as reference tools only to look up information**.

I use the Thompson's Chain Reference Bible . The NIV Study Bible and Life Application Bible are also very good. But see my free report on Study Bibles at
http://www.teachtochangelives.com/thompsons.htm
so you understand why I believe every Bible teacher should have a Thompson's Chain Reference Bible.

What Bible translation should you use? The best translation is the one you will read. I recommend you use the translation that you are comfortable with <u>and</u> that your students are using. It's uncomfortable for students to listen to a teacher who is reading a very different translation than the one they are used to hearing. Many American churches use the New International Version (NIV) translation in English. A recent survey showed that over 30% of pastors and ministers in the United States were using the NIV translation in their teaching and preaching. In 2003 Zondervan estimatedthat over $1/3^{rd}$ of English-speaking Evangelicals were using the NIV.

We praise God that His Word is powerful (Jeremiah 23:29) and can work through any translation. Therefore, I believe that it's simply not worth getting into debates about whether the New American Standard Bible, Revised Standard Bible, New Revised Standard Bible, King James Bible, New King James Bible, English Standard Version, New Living Bible, etc. are best. What a contrast to the Koran, which I'm told by my Muslim friends cannot be truly understood unless you read it in Arabic! There is no comparison to the Lord's Word, which He promised will not return to Him empty, but accomplish His purposes (Isaiah 55:10-13).

I also recommend you pick up a copy of Eugene Peterson's popular translation, **The Message** if you are teaching Americans. (Note: The Message translation is not as helpful for people outside of American culture – the idioms are difficult for them to understand.) Peterson's translation has incredible freshness and candor – particularly for students who have been "churched" for a while. It helps wake people up and spark their interest again. For example, here is Ephesians 4:10b-16:

> *He handed out gifts above and below, filled heaven with his gifts, [11]filled earth with his gifts. He handed out gifts of apostle, prophet, evangelist, and pastor-teacher [12]to train Christians in skilled servant work, working within Christ's body, the church, [13]until we're all moving rhythmically and easily with each other, efficient and graceful in response to God's Son, fully mature adults, fully developed within and without, fully alive like Christ.*
> *[14]No prolonged infancies among us, please. We'll not tolerate babes in the woods, small children who are an easy mark for impostors. [15]God wants us to grow up, to know the whole truth and tell it in love--like Christ in everything. We take our lead from Christ, who is the source of everything we do. [16]He keeps us in step with each other. His very breath and blood flow through us, nourishing us so that we will grow up healthy in God, robust in love.*

Language like this strikes us anew – "No prolonged infancies among us, please." That's why God has called you to be a teacher!

Other Resources

Bible teachers today are blessed with supplementary resources that you will probably find helpful for study:

- ❑ A good conservative commentary (I like The Expositor's Bible Commentary)
- ❑ Nave's Topical Bible (excellent for theme studies)
- ❑ General introduction to the Bible and Bible times (Zondervan Handbook to the Bible is one example)
- ❑ An exhaustive concordance -- every word in the Bible is indexed (I use the NIV Exhaustive Concordance).

I have a complete report available on the Bible Study Tools you need. You can get your free copy of this report at http://www.teachtochangelives.com/toolschecklist.pdf

I recommend purchasing these tools as an investment to enhance your capability to teach. If cost is an issue, then perhaps you can borrow them from your church or local library.

What about computer Bible study programs? There are probably a dozen software packages, full-featured, with extra translations and maps and photos and videos and, well, just everything you could ever want! The ads are so appealing that you may find yourself thinking "Why, if I had this software installed, I'd become a Bible scholar overnight!"

I have the same concerns about computer Bible programs as I do with study Bibles. The idea is great, but all too often people actually spend less time with the actual Word of God. My recommendation: use computer Bible tools for reference purposes and to help prepare handouts.

I personally don't use a computer Bible program, because most everything I desire is available on the Internet. For example, I use the free service at BibleGateway (www.biblegateway.com) to get electronic copy of verses to use in handouts. I don't make recommendations on computer Bible software because I don't use it. (I'm not opposed to you using it, friend, it's just not been helpful for me.)

God may lead you to other resources that are good tools for you to use. That's fine. You have freedom in Christ!

If you don't remember anything else from this section, remember this:

The Bible is your one essential tool. Every other tool must be supplemental.

GBTs follow this counsel. You are positioning yourself to grow deep in the Word because you are depending on the Holy Spirit to be your primary teacher. It is my conviction that if more were absolutely needed than Scripture and the Holy Spirit, it would have been supplied at Pentecost.

OK, let's move on from this tools discussion to talk about studying the Bible.

Prepared Teachers Study the Bible

The Bible is the most wonderful book in the world. Settle this fact in your heart before God, and all the rest will follow. The prepared teacher will be steeped in the Word of God, both breadth and depth. A GBT is competent to handle the Word correctly (2 Timothy 2:11). GBTs align their teaching ministry with the Word of God and fuel it through prayer.

Let us aspire to be like Apollos. "He was a learned man, with a thorough knowledge of the Scriptures. He had been instructed in the way of the Lord, and he spoke with great fervor and taught about Jesus accurately…he was a great help to those by grace had believed. For he vigorously refuted the Jews in public debate, proving from the Scriptures that Jesus was the Christ." (Acts 18:24b-25; Acts 18:27b-28) Some translations describe Apollos as "mighty in the Scriptures" in verse 24. Apollos is a teacher's hero! My prayer for you, dear reader, as well as myself, is that the Lord would work in and through us so that we might become like our brother Apollos.

I believe we need to encourage all disciples – and it must start with teachers of the Word – to do the hard personal work of Bible study and meditation under the authority of the Spirit. God intends to speak to *you*, personally, through the Bible. He intends to speak to your *students* through the Bible. The great Christians who have gone before us have left us wonderful insights and testimony, and we should be learn from them with humility and gratitude. But there is no substitute for the personal work of Scripture study. We can have great confidence in our Lord's leading (see 2 Peter 1:3).

In this section I'm going to describe specific methods to study the Bible in order to prepare to teach well. There are several good books about the inductive study method (see Appendix 1 for recommendations). Following I describe methods that are tested and that have been found reliable, but are not widely practiced today. Studying the Bible in order to teach requires effort and is distinct from the devotional reading commonly taught to believers today.

Important: Your heart must be prepared before God if you are going to study effectively. Begin any study with a short devotional time in prayer, to re-connect to the Lord in purpose and the Spirit.

We'll look at study methods for both the <u>breadth</u> and the <u>depth</u> of the Bible. GBTs need both to be effective.

Remember that all these methods are designed only to place ourselves where the Lord can open our minds to the Scriptures (Luke 24:45). They have no power in themselves. These study practices are mechanical steps we take to be open to the Lord's teaching so that we can teach others.

How to study the Bible in order to teach – Breadth

Many people simply haven't read much Scripture. I frequently meet Christians who have been believers for many years but have not read through the whole Bible. They've heard more Scripture read in sermons than they have read themselves. They don't have a clear idea of where to go in the Bible to get counsel on a situation they're facing. They remember some of the Bible stories, but have not been taught to understand Biblical principles that come from reviewing the whole Bible. This will not do! We desperately need to develop people who are capable of seeing the whole counsel of God in His Word – and can lead others by example.

Reading Large portions of Scripture

One of the best things to do is to read large portions of the Bible or the whole Bible relatively quickly. You can't get clean by showering with a cupful of water a day. Why do we think we can develop a comprehensive understanding of the most important book in the world in small servings? Try reading Luke and John in one morning. Read the Psalms in 3 days. Read Genesis on one Saturday.

Here's a challenge: Read the whole Bible in 30-40 days. Look for themes, broad strokes, and relationships between characters. You are soaking your mind in the story of God's interaction with man. You will find that sin is more obvious and easier to reject. Praises will come more easily to mind, and more richly. It becomes easier to relate specific stories and passages with current events. The interconnectedness of the books becomes more apparent. The Bible – God's revealed Truth – is alive with His Power!

Here are some tips to read through the whole Bible in a short time:

- Don't read for details, just read and absorb God's story. Keep a pen handy and make notes about characters, parallel or similar events, or insights God gives you.
- It helps to partner with someone else doing this at the same time.
- It will take about 2-3 hours of reading time per day to do this, so go ahead and give up reading newspapers, magazines, and watching TV while you immerse yourself in Scripture. (This is like giving up cheap, greasy fast food for a gourmet meal!)
- My usual warm-up is to read Psalm 119 daily for four days before beginning Genesis. This reinforces the power of God's Word in my life.

Here is a 30-day reading plan that you can follow or adapt to your schedule:

1	Genesis 1-39
2	Genesis 40 – Exodus 26
3	Exodus 27 – Leviticus 22
4	Leviticus 23 – Numbers 26
5	Numbers 27 – Deuteronomy 28
6	Deuteronomy 29 – Judges 5
7	Judges 6 – 1st Samuel 16
8	1st Samuel 17 – 2nd Samuel 21
9	2nd Samuel 22 – 2nd Kings 4
10	2nd Kings 5 – 1st Chronicles 12
11	1st Chronicles 13 – 2nd Chronicles 24
12	2nd Chronicles 25 – Nehemiah 13
13	Esther 1 – Job 42
14	Psalms 1 – 73
15	Psalms 74-150
16	Proverbs 1 – Ecclesiastes 9
17	Ecclesiastes 10 – Isaiah 33
18	Isaiah 34 – Jeremiah 4
19	Jeremiah 5 – Jeremiah 37
20	Jeremiah 38 – Ezekiel 14
21	Ezekiel 15 – Ezekiel 48
22	Daniel 1 – Amos 9
23	Obadiah 1 – Malachi 4
24	Matthew 1 – Mark 5
25	Mark 6 – Luke 16
26	Luke 17 – John 21
27	Acts 1 – Romans 9
28	Romans 10 – Ephesians 6
29	Philippians 1 – 1st Peter 4
30	1st Peter 5 – Revelation 22

You may want to read a chronological Bible arrangement to understand the history and the timing of the events. The chronological arrangement makes it easier to grasp the relative timelines of events. Most people really find this helpful in the Old Testament – the kings and prophets, in particular. There are several versions available; I have enjoyed the Narrated Bible in Chronological Order, by F. Lagard Smith. There are chronological reading plans available on the Internet.

Those who diligently apply themselves to reading the whole Bible in 30-40 days will be blessed through the experience. We learn about the tone and quality of God's voice, and the "my ways are not your ways" nature of His working, as we seek the broad perspectives through His Word. These experiences help us fall in love with Christ and His Word all over again.

Consider the experience of George Mueller: "For the first four years after my conversion I made no progress, because I neglected the Bible. But when I regularly read on through the whole with reference to my own heart and soul, I directly made progress. Then my peace and joy continued more and more. Now I have been doing this for 47 years. I have read through the whole Bible about 100 times and I always find it fresh when I begin again. Thus my peace and joy have increased more and more." – George Mueller had read through the Bible over 200 times by the time he died!

Perhaps you're still reeling in shock from my recommendation that you read large amounts of Scripture. Here's another way to look at this. Let's say you desire to teach on forgiveness to people who have offended us. You can read through the New Testament in only 7 days (perhaps 15-17 hours) systematically and cover this. That's amazing! The sad truth is that we have done our congregations a HUGE disservice by giving the impression that Bible reading hard and difficult. GBTs encourage their students to be thrilled with the Bible, the most wonderful book in the world. Inspire your students by your example.

Character studies

Another tactic for studying the breadth of the Bible is to read everything in Scripture about a particular person. Think about how you would describe this person's relationship with God and with the people in his life. Ask and answer questions. Why did God include this person as an example for us to learn from? What are the "chapters" or sections or his or her life? In what ways are you similar and different than this person? How might their life have been different if they had made different choices?

This is easiest with Biblical characters where abundant material is available (e.g., Noah, Abraham, Ruth, Saul, David, Jeremiah, Peter, Paul) but worth doing with less well-known individuals. This method also is helpful to learn from the negative examples in Scripture (e.g., Jezebel, Judas Iscariot).

Word and Theme studies

Sometimes God presses us and we develop a thirst to know more about a particular theme – e.g., *peace* or *grace* or *stewardship* or the *covenants* or… You can use a concordance and Nave's Topical Bible to look up every reference in the Bible to that word or theme. It's helpful to compile all these verses/passages into a single document that you can read at one time or share with others (computer tools can make that simpler).

For larger themes like *righteousness, covenants*, or *God's plan to save the Gentiles*, read through the whole Bible with that particular theme in mind. Make notations in your margins about the theme as you recognize related passages. You might also want to keep a running tally of the most critical passages in the blank notes pages at the back of your Bible, or on a separate sheet. I recommend you pay attention to this theme as your journal, also – God can teach you through your regular experiences as well as your studies.

How to study the Bible in order to teach – Depth

Fact: We cannot exhaust Scripture or draw all the water from its well of meaning and application. The methods described below are specific approaches to studying Scripture (individually and in small groups) to plumb its depths and find specific applications for our lives. Out of these efforts come answers to the question of "How is God speaking to me through His Word today?"

Keep notes about what you learn as you study passages. This requires self-discipline. You will almost certainly forget details if you don't write them down. Also, I recommend you talk with someone else about what you are learning and thinking through – this is an excellent way to practice teaching before you teach.

Praying through passages is essential. **Scripture study unaccompanied by prayer leads to error, self-focus rather than God-focus, and knowledge that "puffs up," rather**

than love that builds up (1 Corinthians 8:1). Our goal is not knowledge *per se*, but transformed lives. Use the "dissect a verse" strategy below, for example, and make these into prayers. ("Lord, please work in my heart so I may allow your peace to be active in me and abundant in me. Do surgery in me, remove anything blocking your peace. Let this be to your glory.")

Check cross-references and parallel passages

Most Bibles have cross-references to verses in the center column or margin. If you are studying a passage in detail, look up the cross-references to every verse. These will show you related passages in Scripture. The general rule is to allow Scripture to interpret itself, and check your interpretation against related passages to make sure they are correct. As a teacher you must work hard to be faithful to the truth – the whole truth of the Bible. Avoid errors associated with building a view of theology on just one verse. (See 2 Timothy 2:15 and James 3:1.) For example, many gospel passages have parallels in the other gospel accounts; these are worth comparing to highlight different facts about the same event. There are also parallel accounts in the Kings and Chronicles that are helpful to review.

Use the NOT method to understand a passage

Another useful study tool is to ask, "What does this passage NOT say?" This approach often clarifies and reinforces what it *does* say. You can use this approach on both familiar, clear verses (John 3:16) and others which are much more difficult to understand (e.g., Romans 11:25).

Let's look at John 3:16a for example. "For God so loved the world that he gave his one and only Son" does NOT say:

- ❑ God doesn't love the world
- ❑ God loves part of the world (e.g., one nation or people)
- ❑ God loaned his son
- ❑ God has more than one son

This is a particularly good strategy with groups of people – invite them to help create the lists of what the passage *doesn't* say – and with passages that are difficult to understand. I have found that students who are generally quiet are willing to respond out loud with this approach.

Read aloud

Scripture is meant to be read aloud. The Gospel is meant to be *heard* (see Romans 10:14-15 and Revelation 1:3). We often learn new things when we read aloud; it slows us down and keeps our thoughts from scrambling off in other directions. Most people can read silently much faster than they can read aloud. But we tend to skip over words and phrases when we read quickly.

It may surprise you to learn that no one read silently before the 1700's. Reading aloud was the norm. The Ethiopian eunuch was reading aloud when Philip encountered him on the road to Gaza (Acts 8:26-19).

We'll have more to discuss about reading aloud in class in Part IV. For now, use reading aloud as a tactic to improve your comprehension of a passage.

Read repeatedly
Read a single chapter or a short book every day for a month, and look for new insights each day. This deep study aligns your thoughts to God's message. For example, if you want to teach James, then invest a week or a month reading it daily. Keep journal entries about your observations. Persist even it seems dry for a few days. Lay hold of God's promise that He does speak to us through the Word!

My habit is to read the passages I'm going to be teaching on at least once daily during the week leading up to the study.

Use the Journalist Approach

Journalists ask six questions about a story: who, what, when, where, why, and how. Use this approach to work through a passage. I find this approach is especially helpful for difficult passages or for stories. I actually sketch a table for a passage, and make notes in it, like this:

Who	What	When	Where	Why	How

(By the way, you can use this approach in class – get your students to fill it out as a group discussion!)

Think like a grammar teacher

Work through a verse or short passage and pay attention to nouns, adjectives, verbs, adverbs, and prepositions. Who is acting or being acted upon? How? Where and when? What is the tense of the verbs? There are no accidents in the tense or wording of the Scriptures, so analyze it very closely as a grammarian! (You may want to check several translations, especially if the grammar of a sentence is foundational to the understanding of its meaning or a central point of your lesson.)

> For example, when Paul writes in Ephesians 2:6 that God has raised up with Christ and seated us with Christ in the heavenly realms, that's *past tense*. God has already done this for us – it's not a future state.

> Notice *who* closes the door to the ark in Genesis 7:16 – it's the Lord.

> Jeremiah is asked to provide God's guidance to the people in Jeremiah 42:5-7 and the answer doesn't come for *ten days*. (How would that feel to us, the "microwave" generation?)

This is a great tactic for getting detailed insights from the Word.

Use a sanctified imagination

When studying a story or part of history, put yourself in the place of the each of the people in the story. Remember that many people in stories are observers or on the sidelines, and don't have speaking parts. What are their thoughts and feelings like? What are they experiencing through their five senses (see, hear, touch, smell, taste)? What would you do in that situation? This is one of the most powerful ways to experience Scripture, and excellent for individuals and groups. When our children were smaller, our family acted out the roles.

As you begin remind yourself that you want to see the story afresh, and prayerfully invite the Lord to direct your thoughts and enlarge your understanding. A key problem as we get more familiar with Scripture is that we think "Oh, I know this story," and lose the humbleness that says, "I can still learn from this passage, today, and every day."

Here are some easier stories to try:

> Adam naming the animals (Genesis 2)
> Noah's family building the ark (Genesis 6)
>
> Joseph meeting his brothers (Genesis 42)
> The parting of the Red Sea (Exodus 14)
> David defeating Goliath (1 Sam 17)
> The Sermon on the Mount (Matthew 5-7)
> Jesus feeding the five thousand (Luke 9)
> The death of Ananias and Sapphira (Acts 5)

You can do this with virtually every story in the historical books and the gospels. This method is more difficult to do with the prophets, letters, Psalms, and Proverbs. But you can imagine yourself in the author's place, or receiving this as a personal letter in the mail and sitting down to read it.

The caution with this approach is over-interpretation, going beyond what the plain Word of God says. There are reasons why God has not provided every detail. Use your imagination, but take care that you do not go farther than is warranted. There is a big difference between imagining what the disciples were feeling as they listened to Jesus give the Sermon on the Mount (Matthew 5-7) and coming up with "The daVinci Code" theory that Jesus was married to Mary Magdelene.

Dissect a verse one word at a time
Select a verse you want to memorize and meditate on. Now read it aloud, one word or phrase at a time. As you say that word or phrase, list all the things that come to your mind about it.

Here's an example verse, so you can see how this works: "Let the peace of Christ dwell in you richly..." (Colossians 3:15)

"Let" *allow, I've got to let this happen, it won't just happen on it's own, I have some part in this*

"Let the" *the, not just any*

"Let the peace" *peace = stillness, firmness, calmness, runs through with depth, big broad rivers*

"Let the peace of Christ" *not just any peace, but the true peace from Christ, "He is our peace," the prince of peace, peace-making is a command, doesn't say peace of the world (which is merely absence of conflict)*

"Let the peace of Christ dwell" *live in, abide, occupy, be a visible resident, actively move around in, not passive or without work*

"Let the peace of Christ dwell in you" *in me personally, in my mind, heart, and body, will affect the people around me,*

67

"Let the peace of Christ dwell in you richly" not cheaply or scantily, but deeply, abundantly, in fullness and power, I can be generous with peace if I am rich in it, wealth comes from Christ alone

… and so on. Plus, you've practically memorized the verse as you meditated through it!   I have found that this method is terrific for personal study and preparing to teach, but it does not work as well for group study.

Creating working copies for study

This is one of my favorite tips – I wish I'd learned this one years earlier! The basic idea is to create a document that you can mark up with your pen, and in a different way than you might want to mark up your Bible. The basic steps:

1. Go online to http://www.biblegateway.com or use a computer Bible. Open your desired section of Scripture, then copy and paste that into your favorite text editing program.

2. In the text editor, format the text so you have lots of whitespace to work with. First, double space the text. Second, set the right margin to 4.5 inches, so you have lots of margin space on the right side to write in.

3. Save the file, and print a copy to work on.

Here's a sample of what the result will look like:

Ephesians 1 (NIV translation)

[1]Paul, an apostle of Christ Jesus by the will of God,

To the saints in Ephesus, the faithful in Christ Jesus:

[2]Grace and peace to you from God our Father and the Lord Jesus Christ.

[3]Praise be to the God and Father of our Lord Jesus Christ, who has blessed us in the heavenly realms with every spiritual blessing in Christ. [4]For he chose us in him before the

You can see how easy this is to mark up and comment! The extra white space on the side is just right for outlines and key comments. (Go to http://www.teachtochangelives.com/Ephformat.htm to get a copy of the entire book of Ephesians formatted this way.)

Now you can really mark this up! You have lots of space not only in the margin, but between lines, too. Circle words, underline, draw connecting arrows to related items, and scribble your ideas about possible illustrations or key points you want to bring out. Here is a scan of my markup of Ephesians 1:

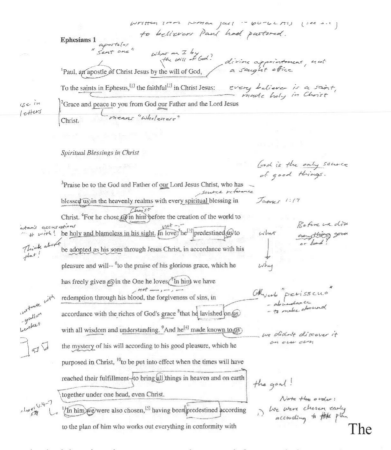

The whole idea is give you another tool for studying and interacting with God's Word. This is a freeing strategy, too. I love holding my Bible and reading my Bible, but I only mark in my Bible when I'm pretty sure it's worth capturing forever. I'm free to write notes on my working printout that might later seem goofy or incorrect, and don't have to worry about "littering" my Bible with useless stuff. I can toss pages and print off a new copy any time. I'll transfer useful insights and comments to my wide-margin Bible later on. These pages are

71

easy to carry around with you, too. Pull them out when you have a few minutes, review, ponder, and study.

Learning from What's Going On

GBTs keep their antennae up and are alert for what God wants them to learn. Study the Scriptures, but also pay attention to what's going on around you. Prayerfully ask God to teach you through any means – newspaper headlines, conversations at the check-out line, prayer time with little children, comments on the radio, *anything*. Years ago I heard a saying, "The Lord is sometimes early, but never late." And I have been astounded at His faithfulness to provide exactly what I need before a class. An offhand comment from someone, or a billboard ad, or a coin found in an unusual place were precisely what I needed. Although I wish He would sometimes give me these lessons earlier in the week, they're never too late.

I could tell you many stories, and I bet you have some to share as well. I hope I never lose my wonder (or my confidence) at how the Lord teaches me through ordinary events.

The key to learning is to pay attention, and be expectant. Pray continually, my dear GBTs, pray continually!

Conclusion

I'm sure that you'll find several new ways to tackle the depth of Scripture. Our gracious Lord and Master Teacher Jesus will lead you. These are great methods to teach others. (That might be a very interesting series of classes for you to teach!)

Keep in mind, dear GBT, that **studying for both breadth and depth are necessary**. Over time you will develop a rhythm to keep this balanced. The last few years I've read through the entire Bible at the beginning of the calendar year, and at the beginning of summer. I mix in a variety of depth approaches through the rest of the year.

As I share this kind of Bible study approach, I sometimes hear the comment "If I studied the Bible like that, I wouldn't have time to read all those great Christian books that are available." My recommended approach takes commitment, and requires you to prioritize your time. But you're unlikely to say on your deathbed, "I wish I had read the Bible less and other books more."

After this study work you've got some terrific insights from the Lord to share. In the next section, let's talk about how to get your students ready for the truth of God's Word.

Part III: Receptive Students

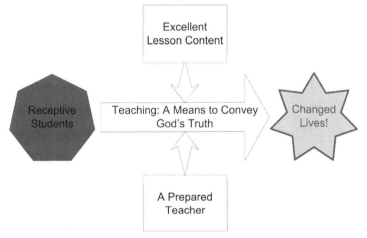

The best lesson and best-prepared teacher can't be used by God to change lives if the students can't or won't receive the message. Their hearts are incapable of receiving the Word, like the seed sown on the path (Matt 13:1-23). GBTs do all they can to make sure their lessons are coming to prepared hearts!

You may have noticed that the 'Receptive Students' box in the diagram has a dashed line border. That symbolizes the openness and softness required for teaching to change a life. This chapter is all about making sure your students have perforated "borders" in their hearts and minds!

There are two keys to helping to prepare your students so they are 'primed' to receive God's blessings through your teaching.

Ask God to Prepare Your Students

The first and most important key is to pray for your students. A receptive heart and mind only come because God is working, and He desires that you invite Him to work. Call upon the Name of the Lord on their behalf, interceding for them. Lift them up to the throne of grace and pray the specific truths of the upcoming lesson into them. Pray for them by name. Here are some specific prayer suggestions:

- Pray that their <u>minds</u> would be opened so that they can understand the Scriptures, as Jesus opened the minds of the disciples (Luke 24:45). Ask that their <u>hearts</u> would be open to receive the message, as Lydia's was

75

in Acts 16:14. Ask that their <u>eyes</u> would be opened to see the wonderful things of God, as the servant of Elisha saw the hills full of chariots of fire (2 Kings 6:17).

- ❑ Pray that their hearts would be changed from stone into flesh (Ezekiel 36:26), and that the Word you help sow would take root, flourish, and bear fruit that will last. (John 15:16)
- ❑ Pray that they recognize sin, and repent. (Psalm 51; Matthew 4:17)
- ❑ Pray that their view of Holy God would increase more and more!
- ❑ Pray against Satan and his followers and helpers, who seek to distract, discourage, and destroy these good people whom Jesus died to rescue. Ask the Lord to create a "hedge or protection" around your students.

If you find it difficult to pray for your students, there is a serious problem. Ask the Lord to soften your heart, show you any sin that is blocking His life in you, and to give you a renewed sense of compassion and power working through you. Do not teach students if you find yourself without a humble, God-oriented attitude.

I also recommend that you recruit others to pray for this class that you will be teaching. Never hesitate to ask for prayer. Your pastors, deacons, elders, and other teachers will be good prayer allies. Don't procrastinate, do this early.

Remind your students about this prayer effort on their behalf. It is wonderful to be able to say at the beginning of a class, "I and many others have been praying for you this week. We've been praying that God would work in your mind and hearts and change you to be more Christ-like. You are not here by chance. This is a God-ordained opportunity for you. I have every confidence that God will use this lesson for His glory and your benefit."

Many a glorious lesson has been prepared but the delivery was wasted because the students weren't prepared through the prayers of the saints. If you want to 'tickle the ears' of your students and have them leave thinking, "Well, that was entertaining," then you don't need to pray. If you want to teach the Bible to change lives, then recognize the limits of your teaching and devote yourself to prayer! I'll outline a suggested prayer schedule in Part V.

Create Expectations

The second key is to create expectations through some good ol' fashioned marketing. Now before you think, "Marketing is not in the Bible," hear me out. You want to create some eagerness for the lesson, a hunger for what God can provide them. The easiest students to teach – and the ones with the greatest life change for the glory of God! – are the ones who come <u>expectant!</u> Here are some practical, tested ideas to help you build expectant students:

❑ Contact everyone in the class by phone/email/Facebook ahead of the teaching time. This is especially helpful before you start a new series of classes. Tell them a little bit about what will be in the lesson – and emphasize what they can get from it. Personal contact in advance can dramatically improve attendance. Even three minutes can make a huge difference in a student's expectations. Hint: script out your key points if you're calling through a class list, so you give everyone a consistent message.

❑ Prompt your students to have some question in mind that they want to see God answer. For example, I recently taught a series about bringing the Gospel into our family relationships (often our most difficult!). I contacted the class members in advance, suggesting that they think about one family relationship that is challenging for them, and that they would love to see God transform by His power. That created some expectancy in their hearts, because they were watching and listening for how God will help them with their family.

❑ If you're teaching the same class over a period of weeks, then at the end of a class period, give a quick statement about what you will cover next time.

❑ Contact class members by phone or email or postcard during the week. Remind them of a relevant point from your past lessons, encourage them to apply it, and give them hints about what's coming next.

❑ Ask students to bring someone else – someone who they know would benefit from the topic -- to the next lesson.

❑ Remind students occasionally that they need to come to class and participate with anticipation that God will give them opportunities to share what they have learned with others. The Lord always teaches us what will be helpful to convey to others in appropriate times in the future. The kingdom of God is oriented towards growth this way. If your students know that they'll be teaching something themselves soon, their attention in class will increase tenfold!

❑ In humility in class, ask your students to pray for you as you prepare for future lessons. This helps orient their hearts toward the lesson and you as the person God is using to present it to them.

❑ Pass out a handout at the end of class that has some exercises or questions to stimulate your students during the week until you come together again. One teacher I know passed out little cards, personalized, with the instructions "Open only after Thursday morning." Inside were words of encouragement and a reminder from the previous lesson.

The general idea of promotion is to help people get excited about what they have learned and what they will learn.

By the way, there are other benefits to these kinds of promotion opportunities. You will be building up the fellowship and unity of the class, and giving yourself the encouragement you need to do a great job. Your class is very likely to grow in size as people spread the word about their life-changing experiences. The kingdom of Christ is built up as we go from strength to strength.

It took me years to understand the valuable of promotion work. My experience has convinced me that **the effort that goes into preparing students' hearts is often the difference between changed lives and tickled ears**.

Ready to go on? Let's talk about practical teaching tips. You're going to get a lot of useful ideas here, and successful practices that come from field-testing in over twenty years of teaching.

Part IV: Practical Teaching Helps

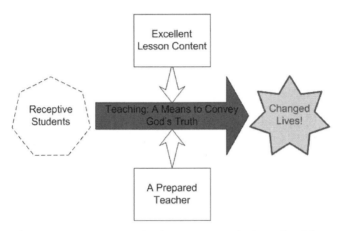

There are many practical recommendations in this section for the actual teaching process. They come from over twenty five years of teaching experience. Oh, that I knew then what I know now about teaching! If you're a new Bible teacher, these tips will give you an enormous jump-start. I'm confident that even experienced teachers will find new ideas here, too.

> "If you are going to bore people, don't bore them with the Gospel. Bore them with calculus, bore them with earth science, bore them with world history. But it is a sin to bore them with the Gospel." -- Howard Hendricks

Worship First

It is imperative that you have worshipped in your heart before you teach. You simply cannot teach the Bible accurately and passionately until your heart is clean and connected in praise and adoration to the Lord.

In a church setting, it's often possible to go to a worship service before you teach.

Or use simple alternatives to worship alone for a few minutes. Read a Psalm. Spend time thanking God for His greatness and goodness, for salvation through Christ, for providing you breath and strength and opportunity to serve Him. Sing a praise chorus or a few stanzas from a hymn that draws you into His Presence.

God is omnipresent (Psalm 139), but He likes to be invited. Invite God to work in you and in the class. Use your sanctified imagination to see yourself as a large and clean conduit of grace and knowledge (2 Peter 3:18) to this class, today. Invite God to pour Himself through you and the lesson material into hearts and minds prepared to receive it.

Getting Started

The opening 90 seconds of your lesson are critical. If you're at all nervous, it will probably hit you right away. If you stumble in the opening seconds, keep going. Students are patient. Remember that these good people are not listening to you by accident – this is a work of God. Their hearts and minds are prepared. You're good, but don't lose perspective – your students are there to learn from God, not from you.

Here are two tips to will help your opening flow well:

1. Memorize your first two or three sentences.
2. Rehearse the timing and rhythm of your opening comments. Your tone and body language communicate as much as your words.

Also, empty your pockets of keys, pens, coins, etc. before you begin. You might unconsciously play with things in your pockets, so take out everything that makes noise. I didn't figure this out on my own. Early in my teaching career, a student came up after a class and asked me to leave my keys somewhere else next week – I had jingled them through the whole class and driven her to distraction! I've also heard about another teacher who annoyed everyone by constantly clicking his ball-point pen for an hour.

Your opening should be strong, and "hook" people into the lesson, queuing up the question "what's in this for me?" Please download my special free report on crafting a powerful opening: http://www.teachtochangelives.com/hooks.pdf

Reading Scripture aloud

It's sad to listen to a teacher or preacher who mumbles and stumbles through a Bible passage. No wonder people think the Bible is boring or hard to understand! Can you imagine Moses, David, Isaiah, Jesus, Peter, and Paul speaking in low monotones?

GBTs practice reading Scripture aloud with clarity and expression. Nothing less honors our Lord.

Few of us have had formal training in reading expressively, but we can improve with practice. This is not a performance that draws attention or praise to yourself. The goal is to be clear and read well enough so that your reading style is neither obvious nor detracting. Do not "put on" a different Scripture reading voice. Consciously read slowly, enunciating syllables, projecting your voice forward. This is particularly important if you have internationals in your class, or anyone with poor hearing. Use your vocal range to emphasize words or phrases, just as you do in your regular speech. Actually, you need to exaggerate your vocal range, particularly with groups of more than 5-6 people, in order to be heard clearly. Be bold as you read – this is the Word of God for this class today!

Reading through difficult passages aloud several times will also give you some added confidence. Special note about those wonderful Old Testament names: I don't know how to pronounce all the names correctly, but I decide how I will pronounce it ahead of class and stick to it.

Appropriate Energy

GBTs are strong, energetic, passionate communicators. (See the example of Apollos in Acts 18.) They connect with people. They make eye contact. They engage people. No one struggles to hear them.

**The simple truth is that you must project energy and
enthusiasm. The larger the group, the more energy is
required to keep them engaged.**

You have to work at it. Move around, move your arms, adjust
your volume up and down. Make eye contact. *Hold* eye
contact on important points. Call people by name – use what
you know of their stories, their struggles, their concerns, their
joys in your presentation.

If you're a quiet person by nature, you likely will need to push
yourself to get to the appropriate energy level. You might
even feel goofy. Don't measure effectiveness by how you feel
about it.

I say "appropriate energy" because there are times and
situations where moving around, waving your arms, and
speaking very loudly are not appropriate. There is power in a
quiet word, fitly spoken, power that can seize attention and
change a life.   The Holy Spirit is a reliable guide on this
matter.

Props Matter

A prop is a physical item that teachers can use to illustrate a story. Good props cement images in the minds of students. GBTs know that props matter.

I used to disdain props and looked down on teachers who used them. I would mutter "If he would use words effectively, he wouldn't need that prop." Two events caused me to repent. First, during one of my Bible read-throughs, it hit me like a ton of bricks how many times the prophets and Jesus himself used props! Am I a better teacher than Jesus, "above" using props?

The second event was watching Joe White, speaking at Promise Keeper, build a 250 lb. wooden cross on stage and then deliver the rest of his talk while struggling to hold it up on his shoulder. His teaching on carrying the cross daily had a thousand-fold more weight because of this prop. This powerful image was engraved on our minds and I doubt many will ever forget it. They will forget a lot of the details of what Joe said, but always remember the picture of him sweating and trembling while holding up that cross.

Two points of general advice about using props with Bible teaching:

1. Use simple props, rather than complex ones. If your prop needs electricity, you're on risky ground. Make sure your prop can be seen by everyone. Don't try to make one prop cover many points. A prop should either cover your central point or be the primary attention-grabber for intro points. Use the prop to help people understand or remember a key point of the lesson; do not build your lesson around the prop.

2. Learn from other teachers and salesmen. Watch to see how they use a prop to make points. What's the timing? How is the prop related to key points the teacher is making? What makes this prop effective? Does the presenter rely too much on the prop?

Telling Personal Stories

Telling a personal story is one of the most powerful ways to engage your students and help them understand the way God interacts with us. A story creates transparency and authentic links between you and your students and testifies to God's grace. A story can shorten the physical and "psychic" distance between a teacher and students (of any age). It's just a plain fact that students are more likely to remember your story than they are some deep theological point, no matter how elegantly you've explained it. Why do you think Jesus told so many stories?

Tell stories well is an art, requiring practice and preparation. Include details to engage the listener, but leave out details which are distracting. Tell stories with voices, emotion, modulation -- make them real. Practice telling them when you prepare. Don't make the deadly mistake of practicing everything else and mentally saying, "Ok, here's where I tell the story about Bob." Be sure you know your lead-in and your finish-the-story sentences.

Here are my recommendations about telling personal stories in adult class settings:

- Keep them short. Don't let your stories overwhelm the time you spend in the Scripture text.
- Make sure they're relevant to the lesson material at hand.
- Test your stories on trusted people in advance to assess their value for the lesson. You might be surprised by

their comments, but better to hear it from a trusted
friend than bomb out during class.

- Balance them out – tell stories about your weaknesses
  and your strengths, about when you've blown it and
  when you've experienced God's power.
- Respect confidentiality issues, particularly with
  spouses and family members.

Let me talk more about that last point. It's fine to tell stories
on the kids when they're very young, but as they get older it's
appropriate to seek their permission first. And you should
clear stories that involve your spouse *before* class; don't try to
negotiate a "is this ok?" conversation after you've begun the
story.   Be sensitive about neighbors and coworkers; use
pseudonyms ("My coworker, I'll call him Joe, asked me the
other day about ...").   Word will get around about stories
you've told. My wife and kids have heard second-hand from
people in my classes about a story I told. (That, uhm, hasn't
always turned out well, and I've had to ask forgiveness a few
times.) I have a pastor friend who used to routinely tell stories
about his parents – until his sermons were published as MP3
files on the church web site and his parents eagerly
downloaded them!

Handouts

If you're going to use handouts – and not all teachers do – make them good enough that your students will want to keep them. Design your handouts so they don't "spoon-feed" but encourage thought, reflection, and application.

Here are a few tips you can use:

- Use larger fonts (e.g., Times New Roman point 12 or 14) that are easy to read in dim light. This is especially helpful for older students, but makes it easier for anyone to scan the page quickly.
- Don't try to put your whole lesson in the handout. Create a working outline, list pertinent Scripture, use bullet points, and capture the key points.
- Leave lots of white space. You want to encourage people to write on it.
- If you are using handouts as part of a weekly series, use content to help connect them. Use the same header (e.g., "Pathfinders Class – Parables in Luke   March 14, 2010") on each. If there are carryover points from last time that are essential to understanding this lesson, put those at the top of your handout – then newcomers or anyone who missed last week will be able to catch up quickly.

- You can make a handout more "interactive" if you leave some blanks so your students need to fill in a word or phrase. I also like to put a question or statement in a text box and leave space for them to write a response. Like this:

> What are three things Ahab could have decided differently?
> 1.
>
> 2.
>
> 3.

Sometimes teachers create handouts with lots of fill-the-word-in-the-blank opportunities. I've occasionally seen this become counterproductive – people aren't listening for God's word to them, only satisfaction that they got all the "right" words in the blanks. I recommend you provide whitespace for people to take notes, but don't lead them too firmly. Leave room for the Holy Spirit to work.

More tips for handouts:
- Make sure there are extra pens or pencils in the room; sometimes even well intentioned students forget one.
- Images and diagrams are helpful ways to break up text and make your handout more appealing. Keep images

small unless they are a primary learning item (e.g., a map).

- Reference other authors, books, and sources correctly on any handouts you create for class. Be a truth-teller.
- Make more copies of handouts that you actually need. You want to have extras for newcomers to the class whom you did not expect, but also to have a few to file away for future teaching opportunities. (I talk more about organizing materials in Part VI.)
- Remember that the church photocopier rarely works right on Sunday morning. Make your copies well in advance!
- If you see handouts from other teachers that you like, borrow from their style and ideas. GBTs learn from one another!

My best handout tip: My files are full of handouts I've made over the years. Sometimes I scratch my head over what I was trying to get across. What was supposed to go in that box? What were the three points for that section? Argghh! So my strategy now is to create two versions of a handout. The first version is blank, but the second version is filled in! (I use MS Word, but you can do this with almost any word processor.) I create the handout with blanks and boxes filled in. That's version 1. Then I color the font for the filled-in sections white, and save that as version 2 – this is the version that looks blank when printed out on standard white paper, and I photocopy for the class. Version 1 is handy while teaching, too. And hopefully I'll be less confused in the future, and can re-use more of my materials!

Involving students in discussion

This is not a <u>sermon</u>. This is <u>not</u> a sermon. <u>This</u> is not a sermon.

A good friend, a very good teacher, has told me that there are only three things to remember about a good adult Sunday School class:

1. Use the Bible
2. Pray
3. Get the class to talk

He points out that they may or may not remember what the teacher said, but they will remember what they said. Therefore it's critical to interact with students and create discussion.

The best way to develop interaction (with you and with one another) is to ask questions – and don't give in to silence by answering your question for them. Ask a mixture of easy and harder questions, those with definite answers and those that encourage reflection. Your objective is to explore the material as a group and increase your students' learning by their participation. Several of the Bible study methods described earlier (e.g., the "Not" method) work well in group settings.

Good information about how to ask good questions is already available online. Check out this resources, or do a Google search for "asking questions Bible study".

> **Skillful Use of Questions in Teaching Adults** (great resource by Josh Hunt!)
> http://www.joshhunt.com/question.html

Watch for signs that the class is "getting it." Stop occasionally and ask if there are any questions. Don't worry too much about questions that aren't directly pertinent to your lesson – sometimes God takes the discussion to another topic. Steer the class back when appropriate or you sense the topic may not be of broad interest to the whole group.

Don't be concerned if someone is sleeping. We live in a chronically sleep-deprived culture. There can be many reasons why someone is dozing off, so do not take it personally as a reflection on your teaching. Do not focus on them or draw attention to them. Do be concerned if several people persistently check the time.

Managing Questions

What if someone asks a question I can't answer? Or disagrees with me? When that question about predestination or post-milleniallism arises ☺, don't freeze up. It is perfectly ok to say, "I don't know" and refer them to a pastor or another teacher – especially if the topic is not related to your lesson. You cannot be an expert in everything, and people who try to be only look silly and draw attention to themselves rather than the Lord.

In my experience, getting outright disagreement with your teaching during the class is rare. Getting feedback (directly, hopefully, but sometimes you hear about it indirectly) afterwards is more common.

If you feel challenged by someone in the class, turn the question around and ask them to explain their point of view. This usually leads to constructive discussion, rather than pointed arguments (Proverbs 15:1). Sometimes a person who states bluntly, "I think it's really about _____" is looking for an opportunity for further dialogue. You always have the option to defer additional dialogue to a time after class.

Sometimes a question from a student completely changes a class, and is clearly a work of the Spirit. You need to be prepared to go with where the Lord is moving the class. For example, I once taught a group of 7th and 8th graders about the Ten Commandments. We were discussing God's amazing love for His people. Everything changed dramatically when one young lady said, "I know God loves me. He's God, so He's supposed to love me. My question is, does God like me?" It was a tender, heartfelt question that led us into a discussion about God's amazing desire to be with us. The class didn't focus on what I had planned on, but began wrestling with a much more important issue.

Life application

When you teach, <u>always</u> leave a challenge for life application. The purpose of teaching must be the application of the understanding of God's Word to change lives (James 1:22-25). GBTs always drive to application. It's got to be about the heart <u>and</u> the head! That's how Jesus taught, and you should, too.

Challenge yourself first. Make challenges personal, attainable, and measurable. "Commit to reading a chapter a day this week," is better than "Try to read more Scripture." Give it a time target. "What will you do by Tuesday night to express practical love for your spouse, your neighbor, or a co-worker?"

There are three fundamental questions all believers must address every day:

- ♦ Who is Jesus? (Luke 9:20)
- ♦ What am I going to do about that? (Luke 6:26)
- ♦ Where is your faith? (Luke 8:25)

(By the way, these three questions make for a great short lesson. ☺)

Don't let your students get accustomed to Bible study that does not work towards changing their life. Scripture is a mirror for us – even the history and poetry sections of the

Bible can and must be the foundation for application. Sometimes the application is focused on enlarging our view of God and magnifying His glorious name. Other times there will be specific acts we should follow.

You can count on the Lord to give you some real-life application opportunities for whatever you are being called to teach. **God wrings lessons through us before He allows us to teach them with any passion.** Prayerfully watch and learn, through first-person and third-person accounts. Be a student of the culture around you. Share with others what you are learning. Journal – and set aside time to re-read your journals periodically. We often miss the longer-term directions the Lord is creating for us, because we're often consumed with what happens today and tomorrow and next week.

Multimedia

I have seen PowerPoint slides and video clips used powerfully in the hands of a skilled presenter. And I've seen technology problems make it harder for students to get the life-changing truth they need. So there are many cautions with multimedia:

- Nothing should distract from the Bible and the key truths that God wants to present. Yes, I know we're in a "video" culture and this is how people learn. I've listened to all the arguments. But if we want people to get the whole Word of God into their hearts, if we want to see changed lives for Jesus, then let us be wary of anything that takes us away from the Book itself. If you can use multimedia effectively to reinforce what you are teaching, ok. But don't assume it is necessary with every class or topic.
- Make sure the technology works well enough that it is not a distraction. It's damaging to burn up precious minutes of learning time fiddling with a computer or video projection unit. Test things ahead of time, and practice transitions. It's probably best to use your own computer, just for familiarity.
- Make sure the sound volume and lighting are adjusted appropriately. Your message will be lost if people can't see or hear it, and will also be lost if it is too loud. Be considerate of your students.
- Skip the fancy PowerPoint slide transitions unless you know what you are doing. Use the same transitions on every slide, so that the students are paying attention to

101

the content, and not anticipating what the next weird slide transition will be.

- If you are using an overhead projector with transparencies, make sure it is bright enough for everyone to see. Make sure your writing is clear and large enough to be read from the back of the room.

- Have a backup copy of important data files, and have them with you. Have a backup strategy if the technology fails you.

Another important media format is music. Occasionally you will be drawn to a specific song or hymn – prayerfully consider whether you should play a recording of this for the class. Music can set tone more powerfully than almost anything else.

Note: If you are interested in learning more about multimedia in Sunday School lessons, check out **eBibleTeacher.com**. Terry Taylor has a generous collection of PowerPoint templates, Bible maps, and teaching tips.

Using small group discussion breakouts effectively

If you are a GBT, then your class sizes will grow. It's good that more people are learning from a GBT. One weakness with larger classes is that people will hesitate to ask questions. Some people get lost in the shuffle and do not make any personal connections with others. This limits the potential to change lives. A powerful way to structure adult Sunday School classes is to organize a large group teaching time, then break up into smaller groups for discussion and prayer.

I think small group breakout sessions work best when the class is more than 20 people and you have a clear application for the teaching. Make sure the small groups are 8-10 people or less. If they're bigger than 10 then you forfeit many of the group dynamic advantages.

The large group teaching time needs to focus on content and set up the life application.
Then the small group time is well positioned for focusing on the application issues.

If you are teaching in this situation, then you must do three things well:

1. Maximize your teaching impact without going over your allotted time. Handouts will be helpful so that people can have key points written down in front of them even after you have stopped teaching. Be sure you have a timekeeper, so that you do not run over and infringe on small group time.

2. Provide good discussion questions so that the small groups can be a successful part of the process of changing lives. Don't allow groups to "wander off" without some guidance or focal point to their discussion. Make sure your questions help the people to think, reflect, share their ideas and concerns, and contribute to a good group dynamic. Test your questions with an advisor – don't be afraid of feedback to sharpen and improve your questions.

3. Identify small group discussion facilitators in advance and prepare them. Try to get more spiritually mature men and women to facilitate discussion. They're not teaching, remember, but making sure that people have an opportunity to learn from group discussion. Talk with these people in advance, and give them information about your lesson content. Remind them to be in prayer for this, because it is a ministry for others. (As a bonus, these are great training opportunities to develop future leaders and teachers.)

There are many good resources about small group ministry if you want to pursue this more. Consult with others in your fellowship that have small group experience.

Praying as the Teacher/Leader

In most classes you will lead in prayer. It's traditional, expected, and entirely proper to close in prayer. Let's talk about that first.

Consider Jesus' words from Matthew 6:5: "And when you pray, do not be like the hypocrites, for they love to pray standing in the synagogues and on the street corners to be seen by men. I tell you the truth, they have received their reward in full." Pray from the heart, with passion, with authenticity before the Holy Lord of the Universe. Either pray a-right, or ask someone else to pray that will. This is not a show.

Pray in a way that leads others to pray with you. Your prayer is a model for theirs. Your students can (and should) personalize your prayer in their hearts and minds.

Leading, teaching, and supporting through prayer is the most important thing you can do for your students. This is *love*. Ask the Lord to give you compassion as He has compassion, insight into the needs of your students, and power to pray effectively for their lives to be changed. The Lord will make you a large and clean conduit of His overwhelming love.

Pray boldly for your students, but include yourself as well. Pray like Daniel, who included himself with Israel in confessing the sins of their nation in disobeying God and breaking the covenant (see Daniel 9:1-19).

Don't mumble your prayers. Pray loudly so that everyone will be able to hear you clearly. Enunciate.

I've been asked if I "script out" prayers ahead of time. I rarely script out precise sentences to include in prayers, but I do think about what to pray about before the class. I'll have two or three key things I want to include. I do this because my desire is for these prayers to have weight and meaning, and be much more than a ritualistic closing.

Please don't limit your prayer to the end of class. Here are some ideas to help you think about incorporating prayer at other times in the lesson.

Even if a class has just prayed over other requests, I will often take 20 seconds for a brief prayer before I teach, or even after I've given the lesson introduction. "Lord, use this time to change us. Speak through me. We are here not by accident, but by Your sovereign power. We need You. Help each of us grow in Grace and Knowledge." Sometimes I will adapt the words from Psalm 19:14: "May the words of my mouth and the meditation of [our] heart[s] be pleasing in your sight, O Lord, [our] Rock and [our] Redeemer."

Paul gave us the command "Pray continually" in 1 Thessalonians 5:17. That's a high standard, but you're a GBT and can pray continually as you teach the class. Let me explain what I mean.

If you have steeped your heart in worship and the Word before your class, you will find that you can operate on two levels. At one level you are teaching. You are speaking, interacting, and engaging students in discussion. But at the same time you can be praying unceasingly for this process. Ask the Lord to give you insights and wisdom to exquisitely match the heart-needs of these students today. You are filled with the Holy Spirit! Pray that the message from the Word of God would fill their hearts. Pray that they would respond for the glory of God. Ask that the seed would find fertile ground, grow, and produce a great harvest. Do not lose sight of spiritual reality.

Be available after class to pray with your students. If someone asks you a question, or even gives you a compliment, take 10-20 seconds and pray with them. Create simple yet strong prayers. If you know a specific need, then lift that before the throne of all Grace. If you aren't aware of a specific need, then pray for their coming week. "Lord, thanks for Bill and your ministry through him. Give him boldness and insight this week." These "micro-prayers" (as one friend calls them) reinforce that prayer is an essential part of all ministry for the Lord.

Short Lessons on Short Notice

GBTs must always be prepared to teach on short notice. It's just part of the job description. Often you will be asked to give a short lesson, rather than a longer one.

Here are some practical tips:

- ❑ Be sure to take time for prayer ahead of the lesson, and have worship in your heart. Orient yourself towards the Lord! If you are really short on time, then do this with the class – simply open in prayer, inviting God's presence and His power to work in all your hearts, for the glory of His Name.

❑ You still need to have a sense that a lesson will match the needs of the students. Don't select a lesson topic based on your convenience. Take this to God in prayer and make sure there is no check in your spirit against a specific lesson idea. If there is no check in your heart, then go ahead boldly and confidently. God will use you.

❑ I recommend four sources for crafting a short lesson from on short notice.

1. Take part of a larger lesson that you already have worked up.
2. Use something very fresh from your personal devotions and study – what has God been speaking to you about?
3. Convey some meaningful truth from a while ago that you captured in your Bible during a sermon or another person's study.

4. If there are current events on people's minds, help them connect these events to the realities of God's kingdom and sovereign rule of the universe.

❑ Aim for 5-10 minutes of lesson time, tops. This gives you flexibility to expand if discussion warrants it, but does not run risks of boring people. You want to leave your students desiring just a little bit more.

Short-notice situations are a primary reason why we want to have our Bibles marked up as teaching tools. There will come times when you recognize that God has given you a short devotion or teaching lesson – mark it as such, and be confident that God will provide an opportunity to teach it someday.

The best way to always be prepared to give lessons (of any length, actually) on short notice is to saturate your mind and heart with the Scriptures. Invest yourself deeply into the Word of God.

"Help! I'm out of time!"

Covering the material you had planned, in the time available, with everyone excitedly participating – well, it's rarely happens. I recommend not being too concerned about this issue. Are you and your students are learning about God and His ways? Then be content.

Generally, your students expect you to end on time – they need to get to worship service, pick up their kids from the nursery, etc. Keep a clock or watch in view and check it periodically without making a big deal of it. Don't say out loud, for example, "Oh, I'll never get all this covered in the 10 minutes I have left!"

Coming close to covering what you've planned is developed through practice and willingness to be flexible. **It's better to leave everyone hungry for a little more** than to have the majority of the class calculating how long you have gone "over," or thinking that you already made that point twenty minutes ago.

You can give yourself "buffer" opportunities. I am usually working on the following week's material, so if I cover an area more quickly than I'd planned, I have the option to work into "next week," even if only to give a strong preview. I also have developed a handful of useful 3-5 minute topics that I can adapt to different situations. It's OK to end class early, but encourage enough discussion that this doesn't happen often.

"Whew, That's Over!" – Not!

Have you ever finished teaching a class and said to yourself, "Whew, that's over!"? Or heard someone else say it with gratitude?

Your job as a teacher is not over when the formal part of class is done.

Let me repeat that again: **Your job as a teacher is not over when the formal part of class is done.**

Your job now is to continue praying for your students, these dear souls whom the Lord has entrusted to you in some measure. Pray that their lives would be changed as they discover new life in Christ. Pray that the Spirit would continue to prick their conscience and reveal to them the way they should go. Ask the Lord to make plain the good works He prepared in advance for them to do. Pray that the key points of your lesson would have lasting impact in their lives. Pray that they would in turn teach these things to others around them.

Let's say that you're teaching an adult class each week. Your students might be getting 50 hours of instruction and discussion and group prayer time per year. (Some watch more TV than that in 2 weeks.) That's it.

Your prayers, dear teachers, will amplify the effects of those 50 hours, by the powerful working of God in their lives. Keep on praying for all the saints!

* * * * * * * * *

In closing this section, let me remind you of the importance of your attitude and presence while you teach. Great Bible Teachers project energy and enthusiasm.

Let me say that again: **GBTs project energy and enthusiasm**.

This is the Word of God, people! We are the adopted children of God! This is not a message to be delivered in a quiet monotone, hands bolted to your sides, feet glued to the floor, and eyebrows under control. So raise your voice, move around, and be energetic.

Your students will pick up on your passion, joy, and enthusiasm – or your nervousness, timidity, and dull heart. The Word of God and the Truth of God are important and wonderful and powerful – let your teaching style match, and you will see changed lives for the Kingdom!

OK, now we've covered the four key elements for Great Bible Teaching. In the next section, let's go over some practical examples for how to put all this together.

Part V: Putting It All Together

> "Life's most persistent and urgent question is, 'What are you doing for others?'" -- Martin Luther King, Jr.

I've emphasized from the start that all four elements need to work <u>together</u> for lives to be changed. You need

- Excellent lesson content
- A prepared teacher
- Receptive Students
- Effective teaching presentation

all working in concert with the Holy Spirit so that people, including you, will grow in spiritual maturity and depth.

How do you put them together? That's what we'll discuss in this section. I've set up four practical examples to walk through this.

Example I: Bible book study -- Ephesians

Let's suppose that you have 20 days to get ready to teach Ephesians to a class of about 30 people. And let's say you get 5 Sundays to cover the material, but you weren't given any specific requirements about what to emphasize in your teaching. There might be an expectation that you cover all 6 chapters, but you're not sure. You know some but not all the people in the class. You've read Ephesians before, but not taught through it.

Even if a terrified exhilaration has gripped your heart, **the first step is to pray**. Take some time to thank our precious Lord for this opportunity to be used by Him. Thank him for these students. Thank Him for the revelation of truth in Ephesians.

Invite Him to work powerfully in your life and the lives of these students. Ask God for changed lives. This is God's work, and your part is a privilege and responsibility to cooperate with Him.

In the coming days you need to make a number of decisions, and get prepared. I recommend you write out a specific plan to get ready. That will help you think through all the steps, the sequence of events, and what you want to accomplish. Here is how I would set up the 20 days of prep time for you and your students.

Day	Prepare the Lesson & Teaching Plan	Preparing Your Students
1-2	Pray for guidance and insight Read through Ephesians 3 times (take notes while you read)	Get class list and contact information List out known needs of class Begin praying for class members by name Ask advisors, church leaders to pray for you and this class
3-4	Read through Ephesians 2 times and look at parallel passages in Colossians Look up information about Ephesus Check Acts passages where Paul was in Ephesus	Start contacting class members and letting them know about upcoming class – get any insights about their needs Pray for students Ask church leaders for insights about what this class needs and recent history for this class
5-6	Read through Ephesians 2 times Make initial decision about what to emphasize in Ephesians	Pray for students Continue student contacts Ask church leaders for insights about what this class needs and recent history for this class

7-8	Create rough cut of material to cover by week and likely focus points	Pray for students Complete student contacts
9-10	Praying for guidance, focus on passages you plan to cover in 1st lesson	Pray for students Relay specific prayer requests for you and this class to your advisors and church leaders Ask God for life applications to give the students
11-12	Memorize and meditate on key verses from week one lesson Decide on life application keys	Ask God for insights into what students need from Ephesians.
13-14	Check commentary if you have questions about any passages Practice reading passages aloud	Pray for students by name Check with advisors and church leaders for insights they may have after praying for you and class
15-16	Sketch out first class presentation details and any handout items	Pray for students by name
17-18	Imagine yourself teaching the class & God working through you powerfully Work on presentation structure, flow Mark up Bible with key teaching points Work on handouts Practice reading passages aloud	Start phone calls or email to class members to encourage them to come to class, what they can expect. Pray that God would pour His love and truth through you abundantly
19-20	Finish and proof handout; make copies Rehearse opening section Practice running through presentation	Complete phone calls or email to class members to encourage them to come to class, what they can expect.

Ok, you're ready to teach that first class. On the day you teach, you want to be sure you have some worship time before you teach, rehearse your closing and opening statements, and invest time praying for students and for you.

Remember, you are God's man or woman for this particular class at this particular time. Nothing is going on by chance or accident. Be bold for Christ! Teach the class with confidence – you have the best material (the very Word of God!), you're prepared, your students are expectant, and you are going to convey Truth from God to them.

The first class is over. Whew! Praise the Lord that people are excited about Ephesians and what God is teaching them! There are 30 expectant students looking forward to your next class. Now you need to prepare for week 2.

You'll almost certainly need to adjust your teaching plans for the coming weeks. That's normal and to be expected. Perhaps you didn't get as far as you expected. No problem. Or something became clear during the class discussion that causes you to rethink what people need to learn from the Word. Give thanks! GBTs are flexible and adjust, like sailors who adapt to changing breezes while keeping their destination in mind.

Check with the class leader or someone in the class to get some immediate feedback that may be helpful for the next four lessons.

Plan now for some mid-week contact with your students – encourage them, reinforce key points, get their feedback. I often find that someone will share something with me after class that is good to relay to the whole class mid-week. This is also a great opportunity to "fill-in" with material that you might not have had time to cover. Perhaps there is some additional detail about a passage, or another illustration.

Continue to read Ephesians (the whole letter) and meditate on the specific passages you will cover in Week 2. Assemble your class presentation outline, key applications, and handouts (if you're using one). Ask someone you trust to proof any written or display materials you create. Practice reading appropriate Scripture aloud. Prayerfully invite God to be working in the lives of you and your students for His glory. Continue to pray for wisdom and insight into His Word and the hearts of your students.

Preparation for Weeks 3, 4, and 5 will be a similar process. Don't miss opportunities to prepare your students and encourage them mid-week. Continue to ask people to pray for you and the class. Adjust your lesson content and teaching plan to meet needs that surfaced in the first weeks, either in class or outside of class time in other conversations.

The main addition for Week 5 is that you need a closer. Take the opportunity to review key concepts and hit those life applications again. Give them takeaways that will "echo forward" in the coming weeks. Leave them hungry for more! Make sure they will be drawn back into Ephesians in the future.

A few more comments:
- Please note that the process will be the same whether you are focusing on just Ephesians chapter 1 for five weeks, or covering the entire letter.
- I've laid out an ideal plan. If you don't have this much time, the process should be similar but more compressed. You might need to rearrange your personal schedule to give yourself more time.
- Don't worry if God delays answers even though you are eagerly seeking God's guidance on what to focus on, key applications, etc. **Remember the principle: God is sometimes early, but He is never late.** You can trust Him to give you what you need. He may

choose to deliver "just in time." Refuse to panic or stop listening to God. Do not be like Saul (1 Samuel 13:8-10).

- Continue to steep yourself in the Biblical passages that you are teaching. Meditate on them often.

- If you are teaching from one of the narrative history books, then set aside time for meditating on the stories and using your sanctified imagination (see description earlier in this book). This will help you engage students and invite them to find truth in the story.

- Longer books or longer classes create different challenges. If you're teaching from Isaiah, then you probably aren't going to read all of Isaiah each day. But read enough that you have meaningful context for your detailed study of shorter passages. Break down a longer teaching project into successive 20 days efforts. That makes it easier to organize your time, stay focused, and not be overwhelmed.

I'm sometimes asked how much time someone should put into lesson preparation. Since this is serious business, about the only definite answer I can give is "more than a little." I think you are going to spend 4-10 hours per week to get ready on new material, including time spent contacting students and others. This is an investment with huge payoffs in change lives. Think about this time in light of eternal matters.

Example II: Bible Topic Study

A topical study is when you cover a concept or theme with your students, rather than one section of Scripture. In my experience students respond well to topical studies because they are looking for information or help with a specific issue. Topical studies are especially powerful if the subject aligns with heart-felt needs. I once taught a series of classes on applying the Gospel to family relationships. Because of the student needs identified before the series started, I focused one Sunday just on the issue of Anger. I was able to pull together Scriptural examples and help the class see biblical principles for dealing with unrighteous anger that is so common in our families today.

You'll use a lot of the same approaches mentioned in Example I for a topical Bible study. Use the same "preparing the student" activities and timeline. I'm going to focus below on the key elements for preparing the lesson and teaching plan.

First, make sure you have a topic for study that aligns with student needs. That requires prayerful reflection time.

Once you've settled on a topic, invest yourself in serious study and comprehension. Do not build a theology around isolated portions of Scripture! If there is time, and especially if it is a broad topic (e.g., Forgiveness), then read through the whole Bible in 30-40 days asking God to show you relevant passages for teaching to this class. Use Nave's Topical Bible when time is limited. Check out related topics, too, for additional insights. [I developed a whole resource to help create biblical frameworks on complex issues -- see http://www.teachtochangelives.com/frameworks]

Saturate topical study in prayer and reflection! You must have understanding. Ask the Lord for wisdom, calling upon His promise to provide it (James 1:5). You must be confident that you represent a topic accurately and appropriately for this class.

After you've studied the breadth and depth of a topic, you next craft this into specific lessons. Here is my recommended two-part strategy to do this:

1. Outline the key ideas and principles that need to be brought out in class. Identify supporting Scripture passages.
2. Reverse the presentation during the lesson. Don't list out the principles and main ideas with associated Bible references. Instead, go through the Bible passages and draw out the principles and applications as you discuss this during the class time.

This approach deals with a primary weakness many of us face – we just want the take-home lessons, and push the Bible in the background. GBTs push the Word of God into the foreground, encouraging students to learn and see how applications are drawn from the Bible for any given theme or topic.

You will want to organize your time so that you work a little bit each day on preparing the lesson. Be mindful of what the Lord may teach you through interactions with others in your life, situations in the world, etc. Our Lord never fails to provide useful examples and applications! A big part of effective teaching is simply paying attention and desiring to have a powerful impact on your students so there lives are changed.

Following is the lesson I prepared on Anger mentioned earlier. The next four pages are copied directly from the handout used in class.

Let's talk about *ANGER*.

- ❑ Anger is very common in family relationships, and usually destructive.
- ❑ Our culture frequently rewards and celebrates anger.
- ❑ Learning how to address anger (in ourselves and in others) in a biblically constructive manner helps us with other ungodly and inappropriate behaviors.

Where does anger come from?
- ❑ Work of the flesh (Gal 5:19-21)
- ❑ Characteristics of fools (Prov 29:11; Eccl 7:9)

Is all anger bad? Test yourself – does my anger cause me to act to save lives and lead me to pray, inviting God's power to save and transform?

What can we learn from Jesus?
(John 7:16-24; 8:33-59)

A biblical response to anger from others:

- ❑ Keep *Imageo Deo* forefront -- pause as necessary, but don't flee
- ❑ Don't respond with same energy (or escalate)
- ❑ Engage at their point of need (heart issue)
- ❑ Engage at a higher level (go to next point higher on arc of discipleship *towards* God!)

127

What about my unrighteous anger?

- ❏ Re-establish perspective (e.g., Rom 8:28). <u>Be thankful that God surfaced this for you as an opportunity.</u>
- ❏ Recognize and deal with idols.
- ❏ Pray. Surrender it.
- ❏ Engage others constructively, focusing on their benefit.

Helpful hint: Imagine
the Cross placed
between you and
whomever or whatever
you are angry at.

The acts of the sinful nature are obvious: sexual immorality, impurity and debauchery; idolatry and witchcraft; hatred, discord, jealousy, fits of rage, selfish ambition, dissensions, factions and envy; drunkenness, orgies, and the like. I warn you, as I did before, that those who live like this will not inherit the kingdom of God. (Gal 5:19-21)

For I am afraid that when I come I may not find you as I want you to be, and you may not find me as you want me to be. I fear that there may be quarreling, jealousy, outbursts of anger, factions, slander, gossip, arrogance and disorder. (2 Cor 12:20)

Do not be quickly provoked in your spirit, for anger resides in the lap of fools. (Eccl 7:9)

A gentle answer turns away wrath, but a harsh word stirs up anger. (Prov 15:1)

Better a patient man than a warrior, a man who controls his temper than one who takes a city. (Prov 16:32)

A fool gives full vent to his anger, but a wise man keeps himself under control. (Prov 29:11)

For as churning the milk produces butter, and as twisting the nose produces blood, so stirring up anger produces strife. (Prov 30:33)

But I tell you that anyone who is angry with his brother will be subject to judgment. Again, anyone who says to his brother, 'Raca, ' is answerable to the Sanhedrin. But anyone who says, 'You fool!' will be in danger of the fire of hell. (Matt 5:22)

In your anger do not sin: Do not let the sun go down while you are still angry, and do not give the devil a foothold. Do not let any unwholesome talk come out of your mouths, but only what is helpful for building others up according to their needs, that it may benefit those who listen. And do not grieve the Holy Spirit of God, with whom you were sealed for the day of redemption. Get rid of all bitterness, rage and anger, brawling and slander, along with every form of malice. (Eph 4:26-27, 30-31)

My dear brothers, take note of this: Everyone should be quick to listen, slow to speak and slow to become angry, for man's anger does not bring about the righteous life that God desires. (James 1:19-20)

But now you must rid yourselves of all such things as these: anger, rage, malice, slander, and filthy language from your lips. (Col 3:8)

➤ **Here is our confidence: God – loving us and being unwilling to let us stagnate -- surfaces these awful moments of anger so we can deal with them!** Let us "sow to the Spirit" (Gal 6:7-9) and reap eternal life – knowing Jesus and experiencing the power of His resurrection in our family relationships.

I went through the Scripture passages <u>first</u> in class. The primary learning from the Bible was looking at the passages in John 7 and 8, to see how Jesus interacted with angry people. I specifically chose not to look at Jesus driving the moneychangers from the temple (Matthew 21) – that was too familiar for this class. They needed to see how Jesus went right to the hearts of confused, angry, self-righteous men, did not respond to their anger with the same emotion, and worked through questions to pull them closer to God. I encouraged them to read through the verses on anger each day that week as a follow-up. The application was to practice the biblical responses to anger that we discussed. (Note: this class was set up with a small group breakout session to allow for better discussion.)

You may have noticed I haven't recommended reading commentaries and books about the topic you've chosen. There are good ones. Your pastor or advisors may recommend one or more. That's fine. GBTs put the Bible <u>first</u> and use other resources as supporting materials (e.g., illustrations, background and historical details, word origins). Develop your key ideas by listening to the Lord through His Word.

Time crunches happen. I believe God permits this because He wants us to remain utterly dependent upon Him and not rely on our own strength and understanding. If you have only a short while to prepare a topical study, then I have three recommendations:

1. Focus on a shorter section of the Bible. Just look at the Gospels, the Epistles, the Pentateuch (Genesis through Deuteronomy), or the Major Prophets. Explain to your students that you've done this, so they understand your perspective.

2. Sharpen your lesson to align to what you are confident your students need – from conversations with others, past experience with these students, and *especially* prayer.

3. Resist the temptation to panic, skip prayer preparation, and find a ready-made lesson from someone or somewhere. This is God's work, and He will provide everything your students need through your teaching.

A warning: there is a great temptation in preparing topical studies to only teach to part of what the Bible says, because sometimes the messages aren't popular or easy. It's easier to "skip" over Hebrews 10:26-31 when you teach on the fear of God. It's easier to blow by Matthew 7:21 when you teach on the Lordship of Christ and the need to obey. Continue to pray for guidance about what our Lord and Master wants you to teach. Trust in His guidance. Do not teach to please men foremost (see 2 Tim 4:3-4).

Topical studies tend to create more "side-track" discussions in class than book studies. That's ok. Pay attention to the discussion – you may see more of what your students need, and that will help you shape future lessons. Guide the discussion back to the main topics when you sense it is time. Interaction and discussion is more important to learning than you getting through "your" lesson.

Example III: Use Prepackaged Lesson Material

The reality is that sometimes you will be given material to teach. Perhaps it's a denominational class guide, or a video series, or a book. My research indicates that about 85% of adult Sunday School classes in the U.S. are using prepackaged lesson material on a regular basis. Let's work through an example so you can see how a GBT maximizes the impact of this material for students.

Suppose you've been given a video series with companion book, complete with background and discussion questions. It's a five-week series, and you have 5 days notice to get prepared. (There's "nothing" to be prepared for, right, so why should someone give you lots of notice?). Here is how I would invest my preparation time.

Day	Prepare the Lesson & Teaching Plan	Preparing Your Students
1	Pray for guidance and insight Watch the video Skim the companion book	Get class list and contact information List out known needs of class Begin praying for class members by name Ask advisors, church leaders to pray for you and this class
2	Watch the video Think about related Scripture that you may want to highlight in addition to the companion book	Begin contacting class members
3	Pray for insight into student's needs. Study companion book – decide what you will emphasize and if there is a life application you should add.	Pray for students by name Finish contacting class members
4	Watch the video Finalize lesson organization – how you will intro, anything to emphasize with additional Scripture and life-applications. What is pertinent to these students' needs at this time? What will honor the Lord?	Pray for students by name

5	Make photocopies of key information as appropriate Check to make sure video equipment works correctly in teaching setting	Pray for students by name Remind advisors, church leaders to pray for you and this class

Note that the pattern of preparation I recommend is very similar to what I recommended earlier for Ephesians – you still need to invest time to discern students' needs and prepare their hearts for this lesson.

Don't be afraid to bring in additional Scripture and personal stories as they add value to the lesson on the video. You have confidence before God because you know your students and what they need. The important thing is that they grow in the grace and knowledge of our Lord Jesus Christ (2 Peter 3:18), not that you stick to the prepackaged lesson plan.

Because this is a multiple week series, you'll need to prepare for each week in a similar way. Give your students your best preparation time, particularly in prayer.

If you follow these recommendations, you greatly increase the likelihood that God will use this lesson material powerfully to change lives. **Changed lives are what count.** Our goal is Christ-likeness. "Now the Lord is the Spirit, and where the Spirit of the Lord is, there is freedom. And we, who with unveiled faces all reflect the Lord's glory, are being transformed into his likeness with ever-increasing glory, which comes from the Lord, who is the Spirit." (2 Corinthians 3:17-18)

Example IV: Teaching from a Christian Book

Great Christian books that can form the basis for lessons, both classic and contemporary. You might have been assigned to teach from a book by Max Lucado, John Maxwell, Chuck Swindoll, Bruce Wilkinson, or Dallas Willard. How do GBTs prepare lessons from a book?

All four key elements for teaching that changes lives still apply. You are still going to want to build on the needs of your students, and prepare them to be receptive. The teaching practices I've recommended above will be effective for teaching from a Christian book. Small group breakouts can be very effective with book discussions – usually God arranges for at least one passionate person in each small group who can help the others because he is excited about what he's read.

So let's focus on preparing lesson content from the book. Keep these two questions foremost in mind:

1. "How can God use this book to change the lives of these students at this time?"
2. "How can this book point these students to a deeper relationship with their Lord and Savior through the Word of God, prayer, and service for the Kingdom?"

First, you're going to need to read the book yourself. Budget time to go through the book three times before you begin teaching. Your purpose with the first time through is to get the overview, some of the key ideas, a sense of the author's writing style and tone, and the general structure of the book. You should be able to do this for most books in 90 minutes or less. Study the chapter titles. Read the introduction and conclusion section of the book. Dip in here and there and read a few paragraphs.

The purpose of your second reading is to go through the whole book as the author wrote it. Be prayerful and mindful of your students. Let God speak to you about key concepts and ideas and practical examples that you can pull into lessons. Mark up the book as you go. Write down any thoughts of related Scripture passages or personal stories that might be important for teaching. (Just as with the prepackaged video lessons, don't limit your lesson content to the book if there is a better option to help your students grow.)

Put the book aside for at least two days, focus on praying for your students and for guidance about the lessons, and then do your third read-through. Your goal this time through is to decide what information to pull together into lessons and how. Do not limit your thinking to strategies of covering 1 to 2 chapters a week. Perhaps your class needs to camp out one chapter for three weeks! Don't assume that you have to cover the entire book, either. Again, pay close attention to the Lord, the Master Teacher, about what these students need from this book at this time. This third read-through doesn't have to be beginning to end. You may spend 3 or 4 days going through the book again, quietly listening to the Lord, going back and forth, until you are confident you have the best material identified to teach from.

Unless it's a very short book, you won't be able to cover all the material in the book during your class time. Get key concepts and applications in front of your students. Refer them to the book for additional details.

Do not assume that everyone has read the book, or even intends to. Some of your students will. But even well intentioned students may be running into problems getting the appropriate reading time. Some people will not have the book at all – first time visitors, for example. Therefore class time and discussion time must be an opportunity to convey the key truths and get applications.

Summing up from these four examples

I'm sure you can adapt one of the plans outlined above to your specific situation. I hope you see how to apply a lot of the ideas already covered in this book and work them together to prepare lesson content, prepare your students, and convey God's truth through teaching.

After your class is finished, you're going to
- File your materials for future use – you're a GBT, so you can be that God will give you another opportunity to teach this material sometime.
- Evaluate your teaching
- Getting back in touch with your prayer support team

That's where we pick up in the next section.

Part VI: Going on

If you want to see revival begin, then draw a circle on the floor, kneel in the middle of the circle, and pray this prayer: "Lord, send revival. Start it inside this circle."

You're a GBT, so you will be teaching again and again. In this section we'll explore a couple of areas that teachers need to pay attention to. You need an organization system and strategies to evaluate your teaching so that you can improve in the future. GBTs reach back to the past and are continually growing to serve better in the future.

Organizing your materials for future use

After teaching for a while, you will find that it helpful to refer to earlier work or study that you've done.

I recommend you set up folders by book, character, or theme to store notes from your studies. Eventually you may need to subdivide some topics (e.g., prayer) into several sub-topics just to keep the information manageable. Keep your outlines, scribbled notes, related articles, class handouts, etc. in the folder.

You might want to make a notation in your Bible adjacent to specific passages that you have a folder or handout for that. After you've taught for a few years you tend to forget something good you already have!

Keep an electronic copy of everything reasonable, as well as paper. That gives you more options for sharing and re-using material in the future. You may want to put a USB drive or CD of your handouts and other files into the file folder with your notes. Then everything is together in your file drawer.

Re-use your materials! One of the great benefits of digital technology is that you can create a "swipe file" of everything good that you have, and then easily find it, edit it, copy part of it, etc – this can save you many, many hours rather than recreating something you already have.

If people ask you for your notes, give them a photocopy rather than originals. Or email them an electronic copy. I

If you get discouraged about keeping sufficient organization, remember that in addition to making it easier to teach the same or similar material again, you are leaving a legacy for your children and fellow-believers. You can pass these along with your well-worn Bibles.

Evaluating Your Teaching

All of us can improve. GBTs are men and women of humility, understanding that the Lord deigns to use weak vessels for His glory. It's important to evaluate the impact of your teaching – that is, if you desire to teach the Bible to change lives!

You need to get feedback from
- The Lord
- A trusted associate
- People in the class
- Yourself

How do you get feedback from the Lord? Ask Him. "Father, were You glorified? Did I miss anything from Your Word that needs to be brought to them next time? Thank you for helping me be part of Your work to change their hearts and minds." Then listen. Listen over the next few days. Sometimes our emotions are running high in the hours after we teach, and the Lord will speak to us more clearly later on. If you've invested yourself in the material appropriately, it is difficult NOT to be emotionally close. We need to have a sensitive, teachable heart.

Every GBT needs a trusted advisor, a person of spiritual depth. This may be a pastor, a lay leader, or your spouse. Select this person with prayer. You want them to be praying for you, too! Grant this person – God's gift to you! -- freedom to provide you with critical feedback and suggestions. Don't wince at their words; take their feedback seriously. Confirm it with the Lord.

Ask others for input on your teaching as well, both soon after class and later on. Don't fish for compliments here. Do not ask something generic like "How was the class?" because most people will give you pleasant but useless feedback (i.e., "Fine!") no matter what they really thought. Instead, ask for specific feedback. "Did I make my two main points clearly?" "Was there appropriate class interaction?" "What would you recommend I do differently if I taught that again?" These kinds of questions are more likely to generate constructive feedback you can use.

Do not look for feedback from class participants about the *content* of the class – let that feedback come from the Lord and your trusted advisor(s). Do seek their input on how you taught and the way the lesson was received, plus suggestions for the future.

As the Lord leads you, discuss the class with specific students. Ask how God is using the class to make a difference in them. Ask how the Lord is working in their lives. Your questions can be used by the Spirit to reinforce His transforming work in their hearts and minds.

Don't trust your gut impressions until you've had feedback from the Lord and others first. You might be evaluating incorrectly. Some classes have not "felt" good to the teacher but were used powerfully by the Lord to change lives. Sometimes that change didn't happen until later on – and it might have been a complainer or someone upset with your class! Again, the issue is whether God was glorified and His Word honored, not how people (including you) *feel* about a lesson.

Creating and Helping Your Prayer Team

I take it as a fact that no lives are changed unless someone has prayed. (Isn't it a wonderful encouragement to know that Jesus is praying for you right now? Wow! See Romans 8:34) Apart from Jesus, we can do *nothing*. (John 15:5) Your teaching ministry and mine are completely dependent upon the finished work of Christ and the active work of the Holy Spirit. These facts drive us to pray.

Too many teachers are just assuming that someone is praying for them, or asking for general prayer support. GBTs never hesitate to ask for specific, sustained prayer support.

I strongly recommend you create and help a team of people who will pray for you and for the Lord to work powerfully through your teaching. This should be your ongoing core prayer support team, all the time. As I mentioned earlier, you will want to solicit prayers for each class you teach. Here is your strategy:

Solicit at the right people. Include your spouse, if you are married. Include your pastor, a peer (another teacher or leader in the church), and one someone younger than you spiritually. This reflects the Paul, Barnabas, Timothy principle. (I know many of you reading this are pastors yourselves. Seek out a like-minded pastor who can partner in prayer with you.) I have found the "younger" partners are very effective prayers, and delight in being drawn into the work of upholding you. And I seriously recommend you invite at least one person from your class to be on your prayer team.

Keep reminding them to pray, and give them specific requests. Your partners need to hear what concerns you have for your students, about the subject you're teaching on, and reminded that you are aiming for changed lives. Get information to them by phone, letter, or email frequently. Report on successes and progress, too. Give them specifics:

* Your teaching subject or passages you're working from
* The key application points that you want to make
* When the class will occur
* That discussion will be dynamic and fruitful
* That you would be able to discern the needs of the class
* Names of students you believe God will touch
* That the Lord would work individually and collectively to open eyes, minds, and hearts
* For lasting change that honors Jesus Christ

Work with your prayer team before and after a class. It's really important to follow-up a class with prayer.

<u>Say thank-you often.</u> Stay humble, remember the One you serve. One of our biggest mistakes is failing to say thank you to those who are helping!

See two suggested books about prayer partners here: http://www.teachtochangelives.com/partners.htm

Your Learning Program

GBTs are always learning, striving to grow. We can't take our students to places we have not been. Therefore you need to map out a learning program for yourself. What should you study in the next two to three years? What aspect of your teaching needs improvement? Where do you need to put in more practice?

Put yourself on a systematic diet of good information. You can start by signing up for my free weekly teaching tips by email: teachtochangelives.com/optin.htm

Here are some resources I've developed which may help you:

Think Wisely Using Biblical Frameworks

http://www.teachtochangelives.com/frameworks/

52 Model Questions

http://www.52biblequestions.com

Basic Hebrew/Greek Word Study

http://www.teachtochangelives.com/HGVideo/

Teach the Jesus Way

http://www.teachtochangelives.com/tjw

Ministering to Tougher-To-Love People

http://www.teachtochangelives.com/NoMoreFrustration

Keys to Accelerated Learning

http://www.teachtochangelives.com/learnfaster

(Check out the list of free resources at the end of the book, too.)

Final words

I hope you have found this information useful and inspiring. I am confident that God is bringing up a new generation of Bible-teachers because of the coming revivals. He wants to use you – yes, *you* – to help believers grow in Christ-likeness.

Our goal is to see Christ working to change lives. Remember what I said earlier about changed lives? *"I use 2 Peter 3:18 as the benchmark. 'But grow in the grace and knowledge of our Lord and Savior Jesus Christ.' A changed life means that there is growth in grace and in knowledge of Jesus."* The path of becoming a GBT and helping others means that YOU may grow faster and deeper than the others around you. Hallelujah, Amen!

The needs of this generation are so great that we need more than a handful of GBTs. We need hundreds and thousands of teachers, scattered throughout the kingdom! That's why I've written this book to help give people a jump-start and enable them to become more effective right away. The methods I've outlined in this book are also designed to put you on a path to consistently deeper spiritual maturity. I encourage you to consistently put yourself in position to learn, grow, and share with others.

I'm still learning how to be the GBT that God has called me to be. God has taught me more about teaching after I originally published **Teach the Bible to Change Lives** than I knew before! I'm interested in hearing from you, also. If you have good ideas that can help teachers, or any feedback about what I've written, please share with me at info@teachtochangelives.com.

Let me encourage you to be a mentor. If you're a GBT, then I assure you that God will send men and women your way who have potential to become GBTs, too. Be their advisory and helpful guide. God raises up these teachers for His glory, not yours. You can cooperate with Him by encouraging other teachers and giving them helpful feedback. Inspire them. Give them help. Buy copies of this book for them. Share what you learn from them as a means to encourage them. Share stories of your teaching successes and failures with them. Work with your church leadership and local parachurch ministries to help them find opportunities to serve through teaching. Pray for them, and remind them you are praying for them. Encourage them to keep looking at Jesus! We must work to build up the next generations of GBTs, as well.

My special thanks to the community of believers at the Johnston Evangelical Free Church, where our family worships and I have tested many of these methods in preparing to teach Adult Bible Fellowship classes. I'm privileged to be part of a wonderful community of leaders and teachers the Lord has established at this church.

May God add His blessing to this guide, for the sake of His Name and His glory.

Glenn Brooke
November 2011

> The grass withers, the flower fades, but the word of our God stands forever."
> Isaiah 40:8

Appendix 1: Recommended Books and Resources

Inductive Bible Study

The methods outlined in Part I are largely original with me (at least, I have not identified them in other writings). More traditional means of inductive Bible study are described in these two excellent books:

> The New Joy of Discovery in Bible Study (Oletta Wald)
>
> How to Study Your Bible : The Lasting Reward of the Inductive Approach (Kay Arthur)

Teaching

Bruce Wilkinson and Howard Hendricks have influence thousands of teachers. Their books are very helpful for anyone with a teaching ministry.

> The Seven Laws of the Learner: How to Teach Almost Anything to Practically Anyone (Bruce Wilkinson)
>
> Teaching to Change Lives
>
> (Howard Hendrickson)

Sunday School and Church Growth

I highly recommend Josh Hunt's material . He correctly sees that adult Sunday school classes are a key element to bringing in and equipping new people for the Kingdom. His ideas are practical and fun. They work.

Appendix 2: Adapting this information for different teaching situations

As I said in the Introduction, **Teach The Bible To Change Lives** was written with adult Sunday School classes in mind. But great Bible teachers (GBTs) can and should use their teaching gifts and skills in multiple situations. The 4 key elements of great Bible teaching still apply. This appendix should give you some ideas about how to flex the material to other teaching opportunities, for the glory of God. We'll cover:

- Small Group Bible Studies
- Teaching Family at Home
- Teaching people you don't know well
- Sermons

Small group Bible studies

There are many similarities between adult Sunday School settings and small group Bible studies. Generally speaking, small group Bible studies are smaller and more intimate than adult Sunday School classes. Use this for advantage – focus more on individual needs, drawing out discussion from each participant when possible.

GBTs have a tendency to get in the way in small group settings because they so easily dominate the discussion. Work at being still and letting others respond fully to the discussion at hand. Take turns reading the Scripture passage. Resist the urge to relay everything you've learned about this passage to the group RIGHT NOW.

Teaching Family at Home

GBTs are called to teach wherever God puts them. Deuteronomy 6 makes it plain that we should be talking about the Word of God all the time at home. Teaching may occur at special formal times, but should also occur in the midst of our regular family activities. A parent or grandparent attuned to the Spirit will recognize many opportunities as teaching times.

Let me break this into *formal* and *informal situations*.

Formal situations might be family worship times, or a devotion at a family meal. Usually you will have some planning time for these. You want to strive for interaction time – even very young children can participate.

The best way to be prepared for *informal opportunities* that God arranges in the midst of our regular activities is to be saturated with the Word of God. Review my counsel on studying the breadth and depth of Scripture in Part II. Keep Bibles handy throughout your home. Carry one with you when you are away from home, in your car or purse. I love seeing a man carrying a well-worn Bible about!

I believe one of the best things you can do for your family is teach by asking questions and encouraging exploration. Study your spouse and children – and your extended family! – and pray for them, so that you may bring to them what the Lord desires.

Homeschooling is a special case of teaching the family at home. There are many, many resources available for homeschoolers. My hope is that this book will be helpful for the specific joys of teaching the Bible to students at home.

Teaching people you don't know (or don't know well)

GBTs are called on to teach the Bible – even to people they have never met before, or do not know well! Perhaps you're teaching a different group at your church, or starting a new neighborhood Bible study, or are on a short-term mission trip, or were called to teach at a church conference event.

This is an exciting opportunity for two reasons. First, you'll be completely dependent upon the Lord to guide your decisions about content, what to emphasize, questions to ask, and to make adjustments once you begin teaching. Dependency upon God is a fabulous adventure! Second, you're expanding your impact on the breadth of the growing kingdom of God's people. New experiences stretch us because of the interaction and feedback that occurs.

Get this in your head and your heart, and build your confidence upon it: <u>You may not know them or their specific needs, but the Lord *does*.</u>

Be careful with feedback you receive in these situations. My experience is that people who don't know you tend to forget that you're full of faults and weaknesses, and so they tend to say and do things which puff up your pride.

Sermons

Sermons (or homilies) are a special case of teaching. I've been surprised by the feedback from pastors reviewing early drafts of **Teach The Bible To Change Lives** – the strategies in this book helped them prepare and deliver better sermons! The biggest difference is the mostly one-sided delivery of teaching.

155

In most church settings (but not all!) the sermon or homily is spoken without requiring responses from the listeners.

Here's how you should adapt my four part plan for teaching through sermons:

1. Receptive Students. I would love to see pastors using the strategies outlined in Part III to increase the receptivity of listeners to the Word of God and instruction. My research suggests that very few preachers are doing all they could in this area.

2. Preparation for teaching. The Bible study methods I outlined in Part II will be helpful to anyone preparing a sermon or homily.

3. Teaching time. Here is where the biggest changes come in for most sermons. My suggestion is to go ahead and think about questions to engage the parishioners – that might shape how you prepare the lesson. You might even ask and answer these questions as part of the sermon itself.

About the Author

Glenn Brooke has been teaching the Bible for more than twenty five years. Glenn is the husband of one wife (and he married 'up', way up!) and the father of two adult children. He is learning how to exercise his gifts every day as he walks with Christ and ministers in His name. In addition to this book, Glenn has written several other books and created audio and video training tools to help Bible teachers. Glenn's family calls the Johnston Evangelical Free Church (Johnston, Iowa) home.

Glenn's statement of faith agrees with the ten points of doctrine from the Evangelical Free Church of America (http://www.efca.org/about-efca/statement-faith) Contact Glenn at info@teachtochangelives.com if you have questions.

Free Resources for Bible Teachers

Check out free reports and articles about Bible teaching:
http://www.teachtochangelives.com/reports.htm

You can subscribe to weekly teaching tips for Bible teachers:
http://www.teachtochangelives.com/optin.htm

You won't be disappointed in the encouraging and practical content you'll receive. Please encourage your friends and church leaders to subscribe, also.

Glenn publishes two free blogs:
Coaching for Bible teachers
http://teachtochangelives.blogspot.com
Encouraging Christian husbands and fathers
http:// boldandgentle.blogspot.com

You can also follow Glenn on Twitter and YouTube:
http://www.twitter.com/glenn_brooke
http://www.youtube.com/user/bibleteachingcoach

Made in the USA
Charleston, SC
22 December 2011

Teach the Bible to Change Lives

Printed in the United States of America
ISBN: 978-1466490802

Learn more information at:
www.TeachToChangeLives.com